D0810484

PREPARING FOR MARRIAGE DEVOTIONS FOR COUPLES

preparing for marriage
DEVOTIONS *for Couples*

Discover God's Plan for a Lifetime of Love

DENNIS & BARBARA RAINEY

BETHANYHOUSE
a division of Baker Publishing Group
Minneapolis, Minnesota

Published by Bethany House Publishers
11400 Hampshire Avenue South
Bloomington, Minnesota 55438
www.bethanyhouse.com

Bethany House Publishers is a division of
Baker Publishing Group, Grand Rapids, Michigan

Bethany House edition published 2015
ISBN 978-0-7642-1547-6

Previously published by Regal Books.

Printed in the United States of America

Library of Congress Control Number: 2015952788

18   19   20   21   7   6   5   4   3

To Laura
You are our Sunshine
You are loved!

Contents

Acknowledgments

After writing close to three dozen books, I want to thank a unique group of people who, if they were honest, stand amazed!

To my 8th grade English teacher, Mrs. Ladd: You gave me the only spanking I ever received in school, breaking a ruler over my behind in front of the entire class. I have two thoughts for you: I am certain I deserved it! and, it all goes to show that you just never know how effective discipline can be! Bless you . . . you deserve a crown!!!

To my typing teacher, Mrs. Whittington: I thought I outfoxed you by typing 100 words per minute (meriting a speed grade of an "A") while making at least 30-50 errors (meriting an accuracy grade of an "F"), which all averaged out to be a "C." This was my goal at the time—to pass your course and graduate. You proved the point that even a student who hated a class can end up effectively using the skills learned.

Thanks to both of you . . . and forgive me, please. I know I was a pain.

And to Dave Boehi: I wish you could've known these two educators who preceded you and bore the brunt of my youth. You would've liked them both. Thank you for corralling all this material from my writings, broadcasts and other ramblings and ordering them into a devotional that will help engaged couples . . . thank you! You have been a gift to millions through your skills of writing, editing and organization. Thanks to you and Merry, a lot of marriages and families have been served well over the past 25 years. You are a good man. Thank you!

To Bob Lepine: You had a vision for this devotional before I did. What else is new? Thank you for your friendship and faithfulness.

To Bill Eyster: You are a good man. Period. You know this wouldn't have happened without you. Thank you for being a friend and world changer. And yes, thanks to his bride, "Spicy" Tracey, for standing by your man . . . because he wouldn't have ever been here without you!

Thanks to the team at Gospel Light for another great job of serving both the author and the reader. To Bill Greig: You have been a good partner in ministry over the past 2+ decades. To Kim Bangs: Thanks for your servant spirit and all the hard work you and your team of Elizabeth Wingate and Carol Eide did.

And to Michelle, who knows where everything is—how to water our plants—and how to serve *really* well. Thank you for being a woman who is not merely a survivor, but a woman on a mission. You are amazing.

Dennis and Barbara Rainey
Summer of 2013

Introduction

Have you ever driven on a big city freeway—one of those with about five lanes in each direction? It can be a harrowing experience. You don't like that lane on the far right, because it's slow—too many trucks and too much merging traffic. You avoid it unless your exit is approaching. If you're like me, you stick to a middle lane—not too fast, and you can maneuver more easily.

But lots of people like that lane on the far left—the fast lane. They are determined to save those extra five minutes, and they don't care about those pesky speed limits. There's danger in moving that fast, but they're used to it—and they like the speed.

In many ways, you are now living in that fast lane. The months before your wedding are a rush of planning and parties and frenetic activity. You live off emotion and adrenalin.

And then comes "the marriage."

Engagement certainly was fast for us. In fact, our entire courtship was spent in the fast lane. Though we had been friends for a few years, our courtship really began in the summer of 1972. We dated for six weeks, got engaged and then were married six weeks after that! We often recommend short engagements for couples, but ours may have been just a bit too quick.

There's one big problem with life in the fast lane during engagement. It's fine for preparing for a wedding but not for preparing to do *marriage*. Not for building a relationship. That takes time and thought and communication.

That's what this devotional is for—to help you periodically pull out of that fast lane as your wedding approaches. Even if you can't slow the pace of wedding planning, it's still possible to carve out some time together each day to focus on your relationship.

This book is not designed to replace premarital counseling; you need to make sure you spend time with a pastor, counselor or mentor who will help you learn the basics of God's blueprints for marriage. In fact, we have a great workbook, *Preparing for Marriage*, designed for that purpose. And if you are really looking for the very finest training that will prepare you for marriage, we recommend that you not only go through that workbook together but also attend a FamilyLife Weekend to Remember® marriage getaway *before* you marry (check it out at www.weekendtoremember.com).

What this devotional will do is offer practical insights into doing marriage God's way. And it will help you begin to develop your spiritual life together—reading the Scriptures together, praying and talking about the divine blueprints for building a home and how they apply to your life together.

We suggest spending 20 to 30 minutes on each devotion. Take turns reading aloud to one another; then answer the discussion questions at the end, and conclude your time by praying for one another, asking God to help you apply each truth to your relationship. These spiritual disciplines will be among the most important steps you take as you prepare for doing marriage together. Also note that there are a few devotions specifically for men and a few specifically for women, but even those will conclude by your coming together to share what you've learned.

It is our hope that these devotions will provide a needed rest stop in your daily activity—a time to slow down and focus on the wonderful mystery of two becoming one.

Congratulations! Doing marriage God's way is really the adventure of a lifetime!

Dennis and Barbara Rainey

I

Eleven *Rules* About *Marriage* that You Won't Learn in *School*

Unless the Lord builds the house, those who build it labor in vain. Unless the Lord watches over the city, the watchman stays awake in vain.

PSALM 127:1

For many years, an email with the outline of a speech entitled "Eleven Things You Will Not Learn in School About Jobs"—attributed to Microsoft founder Bill Gates—has circulated the country. I say "attributed" because Gates never wrote or said these words. The list was actually distilled from a 1996 article written by Charles J. Sykes. Of course, whether or not Gates had anything to do with the list doesn't really matter. The point is that the list effectively reveals that feel-good, politically correct teachings have created a generation of kids with a false concept of reality.

Here are some of the rules of life that you won't learn in school:

- Life is not fair—get used to it!
- If you think your teacher is tough, wait until you get a boss.
- If you mess up, it's not your parents' fault. So don't whine about your mistakes; learn from them.

- Life is not divided into semesters. You don't get summers off and very few employers are interested in helping you "find yourself." Do that on your own time.

Sage advice.

After reading this piece, I was inspired to make a similar list, but this one is entitled "Eleven Rules About Marriage That You Won't Learn in School."

Rule 1: *Marriage isn't about your happiness.* It's not about you getting all your needs met through another person. Practicing self-denial, self-sacrifice, patience, understanding and forgiveness are the fundamentals of a great marriage. If you want to be the center of the universe, which is not a good idea, then there's a much better chance of that happening if you stay single.

Rule 2*: Getting married gives a man a chance to step up and finish growing up.* The best preparation for marriage for a single man is to man up now and keep on becoming the man God created him to be.

Rule 3*: It's okay to have one rookie season, but it's not okay to repeat your rookie season.* You will make rookie mistakes in your first year of marriage; the key is that you don't continue making those same mistakes in year 5, year 10 or year 20 of your marriage.

Rule 4*: It takes a real man to be satisfied with and love one woman for a lifetime; it takes a real woman to be content with and respect one man for a lifetime.*

Rule 5*: Love is commitment, not a feeling.* It's time to replace the D word—"divorce"—with the C word—"commitment." Divorce may feel like a happy solution, but it results in long-term toxic baggage. You can't begin a marriage without commitment. You can't sustain a marriage without commitment. A marriage that goes the distance is really hard work. If you want something that is easy and has immediate gratification, then go shopping or play a video game.

Rule 6: *Emotional and sexual fidelity in marriage is the real thing.* Online relationships with old high school or college flames, emotional affairs, sexual affairs, and cohabiting are shallow and illegitimate substitutes for the real thing.

Rule 7: *Women spell romance R-E-L-A-T-I-O-N-S-H-I-P.* Men spell romance S-E-X. If you want to speak romance to your spouse, then become a student of your spouse, enroll in a lifelong "Romantic Language School" and become fluent in your spouse's language.

Rule 8: *Differences are God's gift to you to create new capacities in your life.* During courtship, opposites attract. After marriage, opposites can repel each another. You married your spouse because he or she is different. Different isn't wrong; it's just different.

Rule 9: *Pornography siphons off a man's drive for intimacy with his wife.* Pornography robs men (and sometimes women) of a real relationship with a real person and poisons real masculinity, replacing it with the toxic killers of shame, deceit and isolation. Marriage is not for wimps. Accept no substitutes. Robbers should not be invited into your marriage.

Rule 10: *As a home is built, it will reflect the builder.* Most couples fail to consult the Master Architect and His blueprints for building a home. Instead, a man and a woman marry with two sets of blueprints by two different builders (his and hers). As they begin building, they discover that a home can't be built from two very different sets of blueprints. [But when God builds the home, the couple will not labor in vain (see Psalm 127:1)].

Rule 11: *How you will be remembered has to do less with how much money you make or how much you accomplish and more with how you have loved and lived.*

Barbara and I will elaborate on many of these rules throughout this book. They are some of the foundation stones of a marriage—a relationship built on God's blueprints.

∾ Discuss ∾

1. As you read through these rules about marriage, circle three that strike a chord in your heart. Then take turns sharing why you circled each of the three.

2. Read Mark 10:6-9. What do you think "no longer two, but one" means in marriage?

3. Pray together and for one another that working through these devotions will help you build a marriage and a home that reflects who God is, His love and His priorities.

2

$\mathscr{Building}$ Your Home on the $\mathscr{Rock}$

Everyone then who hears these words of mine and does them will be like a wise man who built his house on the rock.
MATTHEW 7:24

Since 1976 we've been working with engaged couples, and we know some of what you're feeling as you move closer to your wedding day and this thing called marriage.

Excited, yet apprehensive.

Confident, yet fearful.

Exhausted, yet energized.

It's a mixture of powerful emotions, isn't it?

You feel exhilarated at the thought of spending the rest of your lives together. Life could not be better. It's the best part of the Cinderella fairy tale: magical, romantic, hope-filled.

Maybe, though, you also have some gnawing doubts: *Can I do this? Am I ready for marriage?* Maybe divorce has touched you in some way—perhaps your parents split up, or perhaps some friends have divorced—so you may wonder, *Is it even possible in this culture to build a marriage that lasts?*

We'd like to answer that final question with a resounding YES! It *is* possible to build the type of marriage relationship you dream about—one of intimacy and trust and unshakeable commitment.

As long as you build your marriage on the right foundation.

In the Gospel of Matthew, Jesus spoke about two different possible foundations for a life:

> Everyone then who hears these words of mine and does them will be like a wise man who built his house on the rock. And the rain fell, and the floods came, and the winds blew and beat on that house, but it did not fall, because it had been founded on the rock. And everyone who hears these words of mine and does not do them will be like a foolish man who built his house on the sand. And the rain fell, and the floods came, and the winds blew and beat against that house, and it fell, and great was the fall of it (Matthew 7:24–27).

What do Jesus' words mean to you as individuals? The foundation for life is knowing and obeying what Jesus has commanded you to do. In the Scriptures there is divine wisdom that provides guidance and direction for you just as it did two thousand years ago.

No matter what storms you may face in life—suffering, injustice, tragedy, economic ruin—you can stand strong if you build your marriage on the right foundation—knowing and applying God's Word in everyday life. Psalm 1 offers a similar word picture when it describes a man who delights in God's Word as "a tree firmly planted by streams of water, which yields its fruit in its season, and its leaf does not wither. And in all whatever he does, he prospers" (verse 3, *NASB*).

What do Jesus' words mean to you in marriage? Jesus promised that you will experience storms in life. Those storms will both test and reveal what kind of foundation you are building your home on. And as you seek to build a home together, you can do it with confidence if you both choose that same foundation of *knowing God's Word and seeking to obey it in your life together.*

Many couples today build their homes on a foundation of sand. For example, they may build it upon a romantic fantasy—the belief that the love they feel for each other is so strong, so special, that it will carry them through any`thing. Then they face the inevitable storms that buffet and pound a marriage—storms like selfishness, temptation, financial challenges, differences and conflict, illness, and much more. At some point they realize their feelings have changed—they don't love each other as they once did. They've drifted apart—they don't feel as close. And they don't know how to halt the drift and change direction.

But you can be assured that your marriage will endure as long as you are pursuing God together. Marriage first and foremost is a spiritual relationship. It works best when two people are connected to God individually—walking with Him, serving Him, obeying Him and praying to Him; and connected to God together—walking with Him, serving Him, obeying Him and praying to Him as a couple. If you leave God out, if you push the spiritual dimension to the side, then you ignore the very God who created this institution and the God who can help you be successful in making it work.

It takes surrender to Jesus Christ by two broken, selfish individuals for those same two individuals to truly experience marriage as He designed it.

As Louis Giglio says of marriage, "If you miss the fact that God is at the heart of it all, you'll miss it all."

✑ DISCUSS ✑

1. Read Matthew 24:35 and Psalm 119:105-112. What do these Scriptures tell you about the importance of God's Word in your lives?

2. If you can, share about a time in your life when God's Word provided guidance, insight or comfort in the midst of a "storm."

3. What do you think you could do as a couple to make God's Word the foundation of your home? How can you encourage one another to "hear" God's commands and obey them, thus building your house on "the rock"?

4. Pray for one another that you would make God's Word your foundation, that you would have the courage to continually hear and obey and that your relationship would be, at its heart, a spiritual relationship with God.

3

Marriage Is a *Gift*

Then the Lord God said, "It is not good that the man should be alone."
GENESIS 2:18

Marriage has long provided fodder for jokes and one-liners, and a search on the Internet will quickly lead you to a seemingly endless supply of them:[1]

> "I've had bad luck with both my wives. The first one left me and the second one didn't."—Patrick Murray

> "My wife and I were happy for 20 years . . . then we met." —Rodney Dangerfield

> "Some people ask the secret of our long marriage. We take time to go to a restaurant two times a week. A little candlelight, dinner, soft music and dancing . . . she goes Tuesdays, I go Fridays."—Henry Youngman

> "A man is incomplete until he is married. After that, he is finished."—Zsa Zsa Gabor (married to 9 different men that she "finished")

"Marriage is the only war where one sleeps with the enemy."
—*Ms Magazine*

"Marriage is a great institution, but I'm not ready for an in-stitution yet."—Mae West

I have never considered divorce . . . murder sometimes, but never divorce."—Joyce Brothers

Do you note a theme of cynicism here? It seems that most marriage jokes develop from the assumption that once you get married, every-thing good in the relationship will wither and die.

In fact, it's difficult to find a joke about marriage that's not cyn-ical. But here's one:

A husband had a heart attack, and when he and his wife reached the hospital, he was immediately whisked away by the staff. Hours passed before the wife was allowed to see him.

When the wife finally saw her husband, she was dismayed to find him hooked up to elaborate machines that blipped, hissed and beeped. But she tiptoed toward his bed and, bending over him, whispered, "George, I'm here." Then she kissed him. Suddenly there was a blippety-blip-blip from the equipment. "He was okay," she later told a friend, "but after forty-seven years of marriage, it's nice to know that I can still make his heart skip a beat when I kiss him."

Now that's a little better. That reflects the type of marriage you should look forward to—the type where your eyes twinkle and your heart flutters even after 47 years together.

At this stage of your life together, moving toward your wedding, you aren't cynical about marriage. To you this relationship is a gift—a cause for joy and celebration. Your world is full of color. And that's what God wanted when He created marriage.

If you look at the first two chapters of the Bible, you will find much more than an account of how God created the earth. You will also see that the first institution He created was marriage: "Then the Lord God said, 'It is not good that the man should be alone; I will make him a helper fit for him'" (Genesis 2:18).

Many things can be said about marriage and its benefits for individuals and for a nation, but it really all boils down to one simple statement: *God gave humankind the gift of marriage because it is not good for man to be alone.*

God did not create you to be independent. He created you for *interdependence*. When He gives you a lover and companion in marriage, He gives you someone who will be your partner in everything you will encounter in life.

He gives you someone to multiply your joys and triumphs and who divides your sorrows and defeats.

He gives you a spouse who will help you grow and mature into the person God wants you to be.

And through the children you create, He gives you the opportunity to make an impact on generations to come.

It's true that some of the passion you feel now toward each other will fade after a while (though, like a burning fire, you can stoke it regularly in ways that delight and surprise you). What you will find, as years go by, is that the fervor of new love will be replaced by something much deeper and much more satisfying.

Barbara and I have been married more than 40 years, and we've built a lifetime of memories and shared experiences as we've journeyed through life together. We've raised six children and are now seeing our family multiply with grandchildren, now numbering 19! We've worked through financial struggles and health crises. We've seen God work through us to help build a worldwide ministry to families. We've cried together through weddings and funerals. We've had our hearts broken by the choices of extended family members. And together we've reached out through our tears and sensed the comfort and victory of our Lord in times of deepest sorrow.

Through all that we have shared, we've developed a bond that is difficult to describe, except to say this: It is far, far better than anything we knew when we first married.

This is what we hope and pray you will experience in the coming years, because God gave you to each other so that you would not go through life alone, but with a soul partner for life.

∽ DISCUSS ∽

1. How is your life richer because of your spouse-to-be? List the ways you need the person to whom you are engaged.

2. Why do you think God does not want you to go through life alone?

3. Pray together, thanking God for His provision in your lives. Ask Him to give you the strength and wisdom you need for a lifetime of marriage.

Note
1. See, for example, http://quotations.about.com/od/relationships/a/marriage1.htm, or http://www.romwell.com/books/relation/marriage_quotes3.shtml.

4

The *Year* of *Wet Cement*

When a man is newly married, he shall not go out with the army or be liable for any other public duty. He shall be free at home one year to be happy with his wife whom he has taken.

DEUTERONOMY 24:5

For many couples, the honeymoon glow lasts for months after the wedding. For others, it dims quickly—within days, if not hours.

Some couples experience little conflict during their first year of marriage. Others are stunned to learn quickly that their perfect spouse is not always as loving and agreeable as they had thought.

No matter what happens with you, we can make one prediction with absolute conviction: Your first year will be different from what you expect. You'll find yourself making dozens, even hundreds, of adjustments as you build your life together.

Robert Wolgemuth and Mark DeVries, wrote a book to help new husbands, call the first year of marriage the year of wet cement. "When the cement is still wet," the authors say, "you can form it, shape it, take the ruts out of it. When it dries, you can still change it, but it's a noisy, harrowing experience. It takes a jackhammer and all kinds of extra stuff." In other words, it's a lot easier to fix problems in your marriage during that first year than it is later on, when the "cement" is dry.

Perhaps that is why, in Deuteronomy 24:5, a man is instructed not to have military or public responsibilities, so he can devote the first year of marriage to making his wife happy or, as the *King James Version* says, "[cheering] up his wife." This is not a binding commandment for men today, but it does provide some sage counsel for newlywed couples: Spend your first year cheering up one another, learning how to speak the language of love to your new spouse.

How you start your marriage is a critical component of how you will experience the journey of a lifetime together.

Protect the first year of your marriage so that it can be a time of discovery and of establishing healthy habits in your new life together. Think of it as getting the right proportions of cement, sand, gravel and water in place. Too much of any one component can result in the cement being brittle or weak, cracking under even the slightest pressure. Your first year of marriage should be a time to mix and pour a sturdy foundation and get some very critical habits in place:

- Praying together—when and how you'll do it
- Determining the roles of husband and wife—the basics of working together, who's going to lead and who's going to follow, and how that dance will be worked out in everyday life
- Making your marriage safe—truly loving and trusting one another
- Establishing how best to communicate and resolve conflict
- Setting up a budget and learning to live within it
- Learning how to love and respect your spouse
- Growing together in relating to your parents and in-laws
- Experiencing God together through the study of the Scriptures and sharing what is being learned with one another

These are a few of the fundamentals that, if established during the first 12 months of marriage, will help you pour the right foundation—and will help you to stand strong in the storms of life.

Bill and Vonette Bright, cofounders of Campus Crusade for Christ (now known as Cru), learned the hard way about what happens when you don't follow the wisdom of Deuteronomy 24:5. During their honeymoon, Bill told Vonette that "he wanted their marriage to be a true partnership"; but the fact was he was running his own business, attending seminary, and heavily involved in their church. [1]

> "I was very selfish," Bill recalled. "We seldom had an evening home. I just kind of worked her into my schedule and I wasn't very sensitive about her thoughts. . . . So, she had to fit into my plans. It never occurred to me to fit into hers."

It all came to a head one Sunday when Bill was called into an emergency counseling meeting after Sunday School. He didn't tell Vonette, so she attended the church service by herself and ended up having to wait in their car for two hours, when he finally finished his meeting.

The conflict and brokenness that followed led to a conviction in Bill that he needed "to make total, absolute surrender" to God's direction in his life. He and Vonette each took a sheet of paper and wrote a list of what they had always wanted in life—things like a beautiful home and nice cars. But then "they were convicted by Scriptures such as Mark 8:36: 'For what does it profit a man to gain the whole world, and forfeit his soul?'"

So that afternoon they wrote and signed a contract, turning their lives and their marriage over completely to Jesus Christ. Bill later called that contract "the anchor of our marriage. It's the greatest decision that we have ever made."

Your first year of marriage will result in all kinds of adjustments, tweaks, re-calibrations, and lessons learned that will serve you both for a lifetime. Use the year of wet cement as an opportunity to learn how to "cheer up" each other by loving, serving and showing preference to one another—and by growing together in your relationship with Christ.

∾ DISCUSS ∾

1. Talk about what you are currently committed to for the first 12 months of your marriage. Both of you should list separately your current responsibilities and activities. Then list the commitments that you'll share together.

2. Do you think you are too busy? What can you cut back on during your first year of marriage?

3. Pray together that you can make each other your primary focus during the year of wet cement. Pray for the strength to say no to some activities, so you can say yes to starting your marriage right.

Note
1. David Boehi, *I Still Do: Stories of Lifelong Love and Marriage* (Nashville, TN: Broadman & Holman Publishers, 2000), pp. 141-152

5

Facades and *Storefronts*

The man and his wife were both naked and were not ashamed.
GENESIS 2:25

One of the *pleasures* of marriage is creating a relationship of true intimacy—one where you know your spouse on a deeply personal level that you may never have known was possible.

And one of the *frustrations* of marriage is learning that, even after all those months and years of courtship and engagement, you didn't know your spouse as well as you thought you did!

Part of the problem is that as you date, you have a tendency to erect a facade. Secretly you think, *If my date really knew me—I mean* really *knew me—he* [or *she*] *wouldn't like me!* So you hide behind some well-crafted "storefronts." Sure, that facade starts to come down during the engagement, but it's still there. That's one reason why a couple is surprised at the conflicts they experience during the first year of marriage—each facade crumbles, true intimacy occurs, and the process of learning how to truly love the real person you married begins.

When David and Sabrina were dating, she thought he was the perfect Prince Charming:

> He did a lot of wonderful things, like take me on romantic dates and listen intently to my stories. One of the biggest impressions he made was the fact that even though he was a football fan, he rarely watched it on television. . . .

What I didn't know then was that after he dropped me off from our dates, he would stay up hours after midnight researching professional football players on the Internet and updating his fantasy football rosters. Funny . . . he conveniently forgot to mention that to me!

So she was shocked when, after their wedding, she discovered that her Prince Charming loved to watch NFL football on television. All day on Sunday and on Monday nights and on Thursday nights—football consumed his life from September through January.[1]

How well do *you* know each other? What facades need to be deconstructed? One of your goals during your engagement should be to learn about each other and, in the process, build a solid base of communication. Learn how to talk to each other and to listen to each other. Open up about your lives—your experiences, your family backgrounds, your goals and dreams, your values and faith. This is the time to start a lifelong conversation.

Getting to know each other requires transparency. This special type of unreserved openness is described in Genesis before the Fall: "The man and his wife were both naked and were not ashamed."

Adam and Eve were uncovered physically, and they did not cover up emotionally. Before the fall, Adam and Eve were a picture of true transparency—unashamed of who they were, open to each other and unafraid of rejection.

But after the Fall, "they knew that they were naked; and they sewed fig leaves together and made themselves loin coverings" (Genesis 3:7, *NASB*). Those famous fig-leaf aprons were only part of their cover-up. Sin introduced a lot more than modesty. It also brought in deceit, lying, trickery, half-truths, manipulation, misrepresentation, distortion, hatred, jealousy and control, among many other vices, all causing us to wear masks.

As you work on building transparency in your relationship, several important principles need to be practiced:

1. *Become a "safe" person by building an atmosphere of trust and acceptance.* Major in listening, and minor in talking. Ask questions to draw each other out. Follow the advice of James 1:19: "Know this, my beloved brothers: let every person be quick to hear, slow to speak" Your commitment of love will allow your future spouse to begin to drop the facade, be real and not fear rejection.

2. *Don't ignore red flags.* As you learn more about each other, sometimes patterns or deep-rooted issues will surface that cannot be ignored. Do you find yourself arguing a lot? Is your future spouse able to control anger? Any problems with accepting responsibility? Holding a job? Rationalizing questionable behavior? Don't let relational red flags like these go unaddressed. Talk about them with a pastor, counselor or mentor—now, not later.

3. *Make a commitment to one another that there will be no major surprises after you are married.* Deceiving your future spouse by hiding issues or sins behind a facade can create major distrust after you marry. All major issues—such as past sexual experiences, sexual or physical abuse, major financial problems, viewing or reading pornography, or having had or encouraged an abortion—need to be disclosed and discussed *before* marriage. And if you need help in processing what has been shared, do not hesitate to seek wise counsel.

No matter how well you know each other now, you will often surprise each other as you continue your lifelong journey of discovering true intimacy in marriage, one of God's finest gifts. But the surprises should be only minor ones.

❧ DISCUSS ❧

1. Why does the thought of true transparency in a relationship, in the spirit of Genesis 2:25, sometimes seem threatening? How does transparency benefit a relationship? How comfortable are you in being transparent with one another? (Rate yourself on a 1-10 point scale—1 being closed and 10 being totally transparent.) Why?

2. Here are some fun questions to spark your conversation:

   • How would you describe your ideal weekend? Your ideal vacation?

   • If you knew you had just six more months to live, how would you spend the time? What would you do? Where would you want to go?

   • What specific parts of your work responsibilities do you find most fulfilling? Most frustrating?

   • What was one of the best days of your life? Describe it in detail.

   • What were some of your favorite Christmas gifts as a child?

   • Other than your parents, what adults had the most influence on your life?

3. Here is a challenging question for more serious discussion: Are there any secrets that you need to discuss with your spouse-to-be? Decide on a time and a location that will provide the opportunity to fully discuss the issue(s). Process your response of love and forgiveness. (*Caution*: If you can't forgive, find a godly counselor to discuss and process this with.) Commit to one another that there will be *no* major surprises after you marry.

4. Pray that your marriage would be free of fear, one of growing openness, honesty and trust.

Note
1. For more of Sabrina's thoughts, read Sabrina Beasley, "Help! I Married a Sinner," FamilyLife, 2013, at http://www.familylife.com/articles/topics/marriage/staying-married/forgiveness/help-i-married-a-sinner#.UcnWcuDW6QI.

6

The Seven
Nonnegotiables of *Life*

PART ONE

For thus says the Lord to the house of Israel, "Seek me and live."
AMOS 5:4

If you've ever purchased a car, you've seen the owner's manual. It's the book that tells you about the nonnegotiables for maintaining the car—things like changing the oil, filling the tank with gasoline, topping off the transmission fluid and having adequate tread on the tires. They are nonnegotiables, because if you don't fulfill these tasks regularly, your car either won't run properly or won't run at all.

The same principle is true for the life of a man or a woman who is a follower of Christ. You need to know some of the nonnegotiables that the Scriptures teach so that your life, marriage and family function the way God intended.

In my study of the Scriptures, I've discovered seven nonnegotiables for life. Each of the seven is essential, if you want to experience life as God designed it to be lived. As you form your new life together in marriage, these nonnegotiables will provide a "North Star" to help you navigate during some dark times.

Nonnegotiable 1: Seek God, not sin. God is the life-giver (see Amos 5:4). You will find life in no other. But as a sinful creature, your heart is naturally prone to wander from your Creator and to "seek" lesser gods—self, success, wealth, beauty, etc. Your soul, however, is made to pursue God, know God and walk with God—nothing else, nothing less. It's only as you pursue Him that you find life. If someone were to do an analysis of your life over the past year, who or what would he or she say you are seeking?

The book of Amos describes how God tried over and over again to get the attention of His people. He allowed them to experience famine, drought and pestilence; yet God had to admit, "[My people] did not return to me" (Amos 4:11). But Amos 5:4 reminds us of where life is found. God said, "Seek me and live." A simple, clear command: Find life as you seek God.

Nonnegotiable 2: Fear God, not men. Proverbs 19:23 says, "The fear of the Lord leads to life, and whoever has it rests satisfied; he will not be visited by harm."

Your God is holy and is the Lord God Almighty. When you think of His power and authority, you can't help but fear Him and hold Him in reverential awe. Do you care more about what people think of you than what God thinks? Learn to fear God, and you will be preoccupied by thoughts of walking in His presence, not wondering what other people think of you. You will begin to live your life in His presence and in light of eternity, and the temporal views of men will grow dim by comparison.

The fear of the Lord also keeps you from evil and sin. A. W. Tozer wrote, "It is impossible to keep our moral practices sound and our inward attitudes right while our idea of God is erroneous or inadequate." When you lose the fear of God and don't respect Him and His commandments, you live your life without accountability to God and one another, which results in your going your own way in what the Bible calls sin—missing the mark. Who do you fear? Who are you living for?

Nonnegotiable 3: Love God, not the world. First John 2:15 tells us, "Do not love the world nor the things in the world. If anyone loves the world, the love of the Father is not in him."

What is the object of your affections? Power? Recognition? Hobbies? Self? Where does the world trip you up and try to seduce your heart? Not too long ago, I visited an unbelievably beautiful home; and as I walked around it, for just a moment I thought, *I could have had a house like this.* But I was reminded that a house is not what life is all about. The world seeks to seduce us into a love affair with temporal stuff, but God wants our hearts to be preoccupied with pleasing Him alone.

When I first fell in love with Barbara, no one doubted that I loved her; I was obviously preoccupied with pleasing her. God desires that same kind of singular devotion from each of us. If you love God, then you will do what He wants and be concerned about His mission and His will; you will fulfill His expectations for you as they are spelled out in the Scriptures.

Nonnegotiable 4: Believe God, not the deceiver. John 8:44 describes the devil as "the father of lies." What God says is true, but there is a devil who wants to discredit what God has said and who wants you to believe him instead. God says that "the wages of sin is death," but the devil taunts, "You will not surely die!" (Romans 6:23; Genesis 3:4). The devil wants to destroy you, your marriage and someday your family, so he works to make you doubt God's commands and promises and instead believe him. When Scripture and life collide, which one do you believe and trust? The Scriptures say that "without faith it is impossible to please [God]," but your nature is to move toward unbelief, which is what the devil wants (Hebrews 11:6). Will you believe God?

∾ DISCUSS ∾

1. Read together the four passages mentioned in this devotion: Proverbs 19:23; Amos 5:4; John 8:44; 1 John 2:15. Talk about how you can apply each one to your life together.

2. How consistently do you seek God? How often do you spend time with Him?

3. What would be the benefit to your marriage if you spent time seeking Him together on a regular basis?

4. Pray together that you will become a couple that seeks and fears God, that loves and believes Him.

7

The Seven
Nonnegotiables of *Life*

(PART TWO)

*And I heard the voice of the Lord, saying, "Whom shall I send, and who will
go for us?" Then I said, "Here am I. Send me!"*
ISAIAH 6:8

In the previous devotion I discussed the first four items on my list
of nonnegotiables of life. For a baseball player, the nonnegotiables
are hitting, running, throwing, catching, etc. For you, a committed
follower of Jesus Christ, the overall nonnegotiable is walking with
Christ so that to others your life reflects who God is and what He is
like. This applies as well to your marriage: It was designed by God to
give the world a glimpse of God. And these nonnegotiables are the
foundation of a solid marriage relationship.

Nonnegotiable 5: Obey God, not your appetites. In 1 Corinthians 9:24-
27, Paul points out that you need to exercise "self-control in all things"
and to "run in such a way that you may win" (*NASB*). Your appetites are
the passions that you have within you that are contrary to the spirit,
craving and battling to be satisfied. If you give in even the slightest to
these desires, the enemy can launch an attack in your life and against
your marriage.

DENNIS & BARBARA RAINEY

At the same time, the trivial act of giving in through obedience to God may impact for good another person's life or be the impetus to launch a powerful life-changing ministry. Your passions must be surrendered to Jesus Christ. Ultimately, this is how you as a couple can build a marriage that can stand firm in the storms of life.

Obedience to God demands two main things: (1) the courage to say no to self, no to appetites, no to lusts of the flesh, no to bitterness, no to what comes naturally and yes to following Christ; and (2) faithfulness—persevering endurance to seek God, and to follow His call, even through suffering. Only by yielding to Christ can you obey God, not your appetites.

Nonnegotiable 6: Serve God, not self. If you are like most people, you awaken in the morning and think about yourself—what you will wear, what you will eat, where you will go and how you can meet your own needs. But marriage is a call to serve another person. Marriage is redemptive—it calls you away from self-preoccupation. And, if you are to truly serve your spouse, you must deny yourself and ask God to enable you to serve Him and others. Serving God means that you give up your will and surrender to His will.

At the end of 1972, in the first year of our marriage, Barbara and I decided that before we would give anything to each other for Christmas, we would surrender our lives in writing to Jesus Christ. Each of us wrote out a "Title Deed to My Life," giving Jesus Christ ownership of our lives—including everything we ever dreamed of having or accomplishing. That decision, represented by those two documents, was determinative. It answered the question: Who will we serve, self or God? You need to answer the same question.

Nonnegotiable 7: Worship God, not comfort. In your journey together, you will experience many seasons in your marriage. How you respond as a couple to the wintry seasons is critical. Habakkuk 3:17-18 paints a picture of trusting God, no matter what circumstances you find yourself in:

Though the fig tree should not blossom, nor fruit be on the vines, the produce of the olive fail and the fields yield no food, the flock be cut off from the fold and there be no herd in the stalls, yet I will rejoice in the Lord; I will take joy in the God of my salvation.

Although it is normal to desire to live a life of ease and comfort, when you are comfortable, you can easily forget God.

No one enjoys suffering, but after experiencing many such uncomfortable wintry seasons, we can tell you that we have benefited from the growth that occurs as a result.

Barbara and I have given thanks for inadequate paychecks, for misunderstandings and unmet expectations, for a teenage son who was stricken with a rare neurological disorder that took away his ability to run, and for the betrayal of friends and a family member. Ours is a marriage that has experienced spectacular bright mountaintops and deep dark valleys. Pain has pressed us against our Savior and reminded us that we are not in control. In all these things, we have learned how to give thanks to God and worship Him.

To sum up these seven nonnegotiables into one statement: "Life is all about God."

✎ DISCUSS ✎

1. Share with your future spouse one of your appetites that lures you away from God. Talk about how you can help one another turn away the desire to satisfy the self and instead obey God.

2. Who or what has the title deed to your life right now? Who or what are you living for? What actions do you need to take as a couple?

3. Read together the passages from this devotion: Isaiah 6:8; Habakkuk 3:17-18; 1 Corinthians 9:24-27. Talk about how you can apply each one to your life together.

4. Pray together, asking God to show you areas where you need help in developing a stronger relationship with Him.

8

Marriage Is Not About *You*

Humble yourselves before the Lord, and he will exalt you.
JAMES 4:10

Why are you getting married?

Chances are your answers would include some or all of the following:

- "We're in love."
- "We want to commit our lives to each other for a lifetime."
- "It's the next step in our relationship."
- "I want companionship—I don't want to end up alone."
- "I want my children to be secure."
- "My family thinks I should."
- "Sex."
- "It's what I should do at this age."

I could sum up all these statements in one sentence: Most people get married because they want to be happy. And on one level, there's nothing wrong with that. When God brings two people together in marriage, it is a happy and joyful event. He means it for good in their lives.

But on another level, marriage will never work if it's all about you and your happiness.

In the previous two devotions I wrote about the nonnegotiables of life, and they all focused on God. Life is not about you—it's about God. It's about who He is. It's about His purposes and what He is up to on planet Earth. All this also applies directly to your marriage.

That's what Derrick and Maria Purcell discovered, though I wouldn't recommend the path they took. They thought they had set up their marriage well. Maria writes:

> Dating Derrick was a joy. We not only spent time getting to know each other, but also attended church events together and participated in community outreach projects. His proposal was planned and very romantic. We prepared a marriage ceremony and reception that gave God the glory, and we thought that our life together would be great.

Like so many couples in marriage, they were soon surprised to learn how selfish they each were. And a marriage based on happiness doesn't work when your spouse's self-centered idea of happiness is different from your self-centered idea. Maria's marriage was a case in point:

> Derrick had the "I am the king of this house and you will serve me" syndrome. After being single for 33 years, he wanted all of the attention on himself. His parents had always praised him and he expected the same from me. He said that he felt like he received more respect at work and from friends than he did at home.
>
> I had been a single mom for years and had worked hard raising my girls all alone. I wanted to be "queen of the house" and felt like my king should serve me. I thought I deserved this after doing things for myself and everyone else for so

long. I wanted Derrick to do life my way while pampering and spoiling me.

We didn't recognize God in our marriage, but pretended it was perfect when we were in front of our friends or at church. We lived more as roommates and didn't know how to compromise. Working at marriage was foreign to us. We thought since we were Christians, marriage would just work itself out.

Neither of us was willing to budge—we were both very stubborn and selfish.

After four years of struggle, Maria heard about FamilyLife's Weekend to Remember marriage getaways. They decided to attend. She figured Derrick would learn that he was the reason their marriage wasn't working, but he told her, "Now you will see that I am right and you are wrong."

Instead, they learned that both of them were at fault. "We learned that we were each other's gift from God and that the Lord needed to be at the center of our relationship." They understood their need to set aside their selfish desires and commit their lives and marriage to Christ.

In serving the Lord I've learned to serve my husband. I've learned to accept Derrick unconditionally and now allow him to be the man of God and the leader of our home that God has called him to be. In doing this I not only gained a husband, but also gained a friend. I had to let go of myself to receive what the Lord had for me. . . .

Sometimes I sit back and think, *My God, I cannot believe that we have come this far.* Derrick and I were two very strong-willed people who just would not budge. But now we have the tools to make our marriage work. We've learned to do marriage God's way.

Derrick and Maria saw their marriage change when they realized that their marriage had a bigger purpose than their happiness, and they humbled themselves before God.

∾ DISCUSS ∾

1. Derrick and Maria attended church together before they were married, and they "gave God the glory" on their wedding day, but she then admits that they "didn't recognize God in [their] marriage." What do you think she meant? How did their attitude about God's role in their lives and marriage change?

2. Read James 4:4-10. What does this passage say about the reasons people quarrel with one another? What does it say about the solution to quarrels?

3. Discuss the wisdom in attending and experiencing a Weekend to Remember both *before and after you get married*. See www.familylife.com/weekendtoremember for details.

4. Pray together and for one another that God will give you each the wisdom to see the need to continually humble yourself before God in your marriage.

9

A *Grander* Plan

Oh, magnify the Lord with me, and let us exalt his name together.
PSALM 34:3

Did you know that the Bible actually begins and ends with a marriage?

Those of us who grew up in church were taught that that the beginning of Genesis describes how God created the heavens and the earth. But something critical happens at the end of that creation sequence: God establishes marriage as a foundational institution for the human race.

As I discussed in the last devotion, marriage will not work if it is built around your happiness. You will begin to understand that at some point during your first years of marriage. And then, if you are willing to listen to the wisdom of the Scriptures, you will learn that God's purposes for marriage are far grander, far more noble and important, and far *better* than you can have imagined.

The first two chapters of Genesis include two key passages that discuss God's purposes for marriage. The first mention of marriage is in Genesis 1:27-28:

> So God created man in his own image, in the image of God he created him; male and female he created them. And God blessed them. And God said to them, "Be fruitful and multiply and fill the earth."

In this passage we see that God created humans in His image. In a mysterious way, the relationship between a man and a woman in marriage is meant *to mirror God's image.* When people look at your marriage relationship, they should see God at work. Your marriage should reflect God's image to a world that desperately needs to see who He is and what He is doing.

That's a hard concept to grasp, isn't it? Think of it this way: When people see you love and serve each other despite your faults, they see a glimpse of God's unconditional love. When they see you forgive each other, they see a sliver of the forgiveness that God extends to us. The relationship between a man and a woman in marriage is a reflection of Christ's relationship with the Church.

Also note that God commanded humans to "be fruitful and multiply." One of His purposes for marriage is *to leave a godly legacy through children.* God created the family as a unique institution for passing the truth about Him and the experience of Him from generation to generation (see Deuteronomy 6:5-7; Psalm 78:5-7). Teaching your children about God may very well be some of the most important work you do together as a couple.

In Genesis 2:18 we learn more about marriage:

Then the Lord God said, "It is not good that the man should be alone; I will make him a helper fit for him."

This passage outlines a third reason God created marriage: *to have the couple mutually complete each other.*

It's fascinating to see how often God brings opposites together in marriage. An extrovert marries an introvert. A task-oriented person marries someone who is people-oriented. A night person marries a morning person. Then there are differences in skills, family backgrounds, life experiences, values, spiritual maturity, and much more.

As you look at your relationship heading into marriage, you see these differences and marvel at how you just seem to fit together, like two halves of a torn photograph finally reunited. This is one of the strange and wonderful aspects of marriage—how God brings two very different people together and makes them stronger as a team than they were as individuals.

When Barbara and I married, I knew she was the one for me, because I sensed that she could complete me as well as be a wonderful companion. But now, after over 41 years of serving God together—as suggested in Psalm 34:3—I really appreciate the genius of how God custom-made her for me. I cannot imagine what kind of man I would be today without Barbara.

∾ DISCUSS ∾

1. Read Psalm 34:1-3. What do you think "magnify the Lord . . . together" means for you two? How will you better magnify God as a couple, rather than just individually?
2. What is your perspective about children? What has impacted your attitudes about them? What do you think about God's command to "be fruitful and multiply" (Genesis 1:28)?
3. This should be fun: Individually make a list 10 ways you are different from each other. Then get together, share your lists, and discuss how you have seen God use you to complete each other.
4. Take turns thanking God for one another and pray together that God would bring you to a deeper understanding of how He has brought you together and how He will use you to reflect His image.

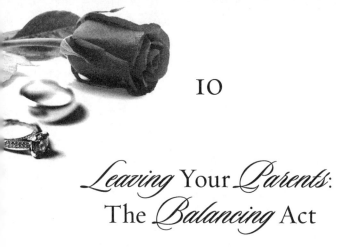

10

Leaving Your Parents: The Balancing Act

Therefore a man shall leave his father and his mother.
GENESIS 2:24

A few weeks after their wedding, a young husband came home to find his wife in tears. She told him that his father had called her and said, "I cannot believe you forgot my wife's birthday." In the father's mind, it was her responsibility to keep up with such occasions like these—even birthdays for her in-laws.

The young man knew what he had to do. First he got on the phone with his mother and said, "Mom, I want to apologize for not sending you a birthday card or present. I'm really sorry about that." Then he asked to talk with his father.

"Dad, this is the only time I want to have this conversation with you," the young man said sternly but respectfully. "I never want you to do that to my wife again. My loyalty now is to her, and if you have a problem with something I have done, then you need to talk to *me*."

I wonder how many young husbands would have stepped up with that type of courage in similar circumstances. What impresses me is that not only did the new husband honor his mother through his apology, but he also did not hesitate to let his father know that he (the father) had overstepped his boundaries. And in the process the young husband let his new bride know that she was the new priority in his life.

When you marry, you face a difficult balancing act with your parents. On one hand, you have the fifth of the Ten Commandments: "Honor your father and your mother, that your days may be long in the land that the Lord your God is giving you" (Exodus 20:12). No matter what your age, you should honor your parents by spending time with them, thanking them for what they've done well, caring for them as necessary and, yes, remembering their birthdays!

On the other hand, you have Genesis 2:24, part of the narrative where God creates the institution of marriage: "Therefore a man shall leave his father and his mother and hold fast to his wife; and they shall become one flesh." The Hebrew word translated here as "leave" means to forsake dependence upon, to leave behind, to literally let go. As difficult as it may be, when you marry, you declare to the world, "No other person on earth is more important to me than my spouse." Your spouse becomes a higher priority than your parents.

So how do you balance leaving your parents while also honoring them? Here are a few suggestions:

1. *When you marry, if at all possible, set up your own home and family.* This means more than physically living apart from your parents; it also involves setting your own schedule, creating your own family traditions, and establishing your own values and priorities—among other things.

   Early in marriage, one of the most common points of conflict with in-laws is holidays. Where will you spend Thanksgiving, Christmas, Easter or other occasions? It is difficult for many to accept the fact that those holidays will never be the same as they were. Well ahead of these occasions, talk about expectations and possibilities with your parents. Be creative and flexible, and guide your parents to be the same.

2. *Sever all dependence on your parents.* One of the most common problems a newly married couple faces is allowing parents to bail them out of financial difficulty. I know of one couple that kept turning to the wife's parents to bail them out after a series of poor financial choices. As a result, the husband was not forced to step up to his responsibility to provide for his family and to live with the consequences of poor choices. It undermined his self-respect as a man, and his wife lost her respect for him as well.

It's also important to sever emotional dependence. Some spouses are so accustomed to consulting their parents, for example, that they feel uncomfortable making decisions on their own. There's nothing wrong with getting advice and wise counsel from your parents. The problem comes when either you consider your parent's opinion so important that you follow their advice only to please them or you lack confidence in your ability to make good decisions independently. Learn how to lean upon one another, and make decisions prayerfully as a couple.

3. *Look for opportunities to spend time with your parents.* Leaving does not mean total withdrawal from your parents relationally; that's abandonment, not leaving. If they live fairly close by, look for ways for you as a couple to spend time together with them throughout the year—an extended weekend, an occasional dinner or a visit to your new apartment or house.

If your parents live far away, you will need to make a special effort to visit them on a regular basis during weekends, vacations, etc. This will involve flexibility and sacrifice, but that's part of what family is all about.

4. *Don't allow your parents to manipulate you.* Manipulation by parents is one of the most difficult issues to address. Your parents know you well, and they know what buttons to push so that you will do what they want. Sometimes they don't even realize how they are being manipulative. If you run into this problem, first seek counsel from an older couple who may have ideas about how to easily resolve the issue. If need be, lovingly establish boundaries to establish your independence.

5. *Protect each other.* Don't criticize your spouse to your parents or share how your spouse has failed. If you are having a conflict with your spouse, don't get advice from your parents.

I once made the mistake of making a negative comment about Barbara to my mother. It was not a major issue, and I soon forgot it—but my mom didn't. For years she brought up that comment occasionally, and I realized that I had not protected Barbara as I should have.

For many of you, the act of leaving your parents will be one of the most challenging steps of your life. But it's a vital step in the process of growing up and establishing your own home.

∽ DISCUSS ∽

1. As you approach your wedding, in what ways do you think leaving your parents will be difficult for you? For them? What issues have already come up?

2. Sometime before your wedding, meet with your parents and talk about the issue of your leaving home. Discuss their expectations—and your expectations—once you leave.

3. Discuss the possibility of writing tributes to honor your parents, framing the tributes and reading them to your parents at the rehearsal dinner or wedding reception. (For help writing a tribute, check out "The Greatest Gift You'll Ever Give Your Parents" at www.familylife.com.)

4. Pray for your parents as you begin a new relationship with them in this new season of life. Pray together that God will give you insight into how to leave your parents well and with honor. Pray that you will have the strength to lovingly confront them if necessary.

II

Till *Death* Do Us *Part*

BY BARBARA RAINEY

What therefore God has joined together, let not man separate.
MARK 10:9

For over a century many have been captivated by the story of the Titanic—the gigantic, "unsinkable" ocean liner that hit an iceberg on its maiden voyage and sank on April 15, 1912. Of all the stories from that fateful night, perhaps my favorite is of Isidor and Ida Straus, the elderly owners of Macy's department store in New York City.

As the Titanic was sinking, Isidor and Ida stood in line for the lifeboats. But there was not enough space for all aboard, and priority was given to women, children and the elderly. When Isidor declared he would not board a lifeboat until the other men did, Ida refused to leave his side. He urged her to save herself, but she is reported to have said, "We have lived together many years. Where you go, I go."

And so they died together. Isidor's body was later found, but Ida's was lost. In a cemetery in the Bronx, a monument dedicated to both of them has on it these words: "Many waters cannot quench love, neither can the floods drown it" (Solomon 8:7, *KJV*).

Somehow the drama of Ida's love and devotion has captured the public's imagination through the years. In an age when so many marriages end in divorce, this story of unbreakable commitment strikes a chord—it is what we long for when we marry.

In the last devotion we looked at Genesis 2:24, part of the narrative of God establishing the institution of marriage. I like the phrasing of that Scripture in the *King James Version*: "Therefore shall a man leave his father and his mother, and shall cleave unto his wife: and they shall be one flesh." In this context, "cleave" means to adhere, to stick fast.

The marriage ceremony is a symbol of "leaving and cleaving." A father walks the bride up the aisle and leaves her after giving her to the groom; then the couple repeats their vows, declaring to God and to their friends and family that they will cleave to each other as husband and wife for a lifetime—"for better, for worse . . . for richer, for poorer . . . in sickness and in health . . . forsaking all others . . . 'till death do us part."

For a true follower of Jesus Christ, this is the most sacred commitment two people ever make. As Jesus remarked, "What therefore God has joined together, let not man separate" (Mark 10:9). This commitment is truly a step of faith, because most couples on their wedding day have little understanding of how this commitment will be tested. That certainly was true of Dennis and me. After years of marriage, we have known more days of joy and profound love than we can count, but on our wedding day how were we to know about the *other* sorts of days?

We didn't know about the days when our budget would be strained. We didn't know about the days when those differences in personality that seemed so attractive during our courtship and engagement would become the fuel for countless arguments. We didn't know about the serious health issues I would face. We didn't know we would have six children, each with his or her own sufferings that we the parents felt intensely. We didn't know about the dark days when our hearts would be broken.

On our wedding day, we didn't understand that we were committing to love, not only the person standing across from us, but also the person *each would become*. That is the great unknown of marriage.

We've never considered divorce, not because we didn't have problems difficult enough to warrant it, but because we decided from the beginning that it wasn't an option. Our conviction has always been that God had called us together; therefore, with His help we would find a way through each crisis, knowing He can and will bring good to us if we keep believing and don't quit.

I hope and pray that this is your mutual conviction, too, as your wedding day nears. You both must make this decision. You can't know today if you have the ability to fulfill the vows you're about to make, but you can know that God will give you the strength to accomplish whatever He calls you to, for He has said, "Nothing is too difficult for Me" (see Jeremiah 32:27). Has God called the two of you together? Then believe that He will give both of you the strength and perseverance you need to fulfill His calling.

There is an incredible security in knowing that no matter what happens, your spouse will be there by your side, till death do you part. After more than 4 decades of knowing that security, I can't imagine life without it.

∽ DISCUSS ∽

1. Make a list of what you have seen or experienced that has shown you that God has called you together, so you can remember the truth of His leading in the hard times to come.

2. Read Ephesians 3:14-21. How can you apply this passage to the journey you are about to begin on your wedding day?

3. How do we both feel about the commitment we are about to make to one another and God? Discuss if divorce will ever be an option.

4. Pray together for the strength that God promises. Pray that God does far more abundantly than all you could ask or think, "according to the power at work within us" (Ephesians 3:20).

12

Sex Outside of *Marriage*: Where *Life* and *Truth* Collide

Abstain from sexual immorality.
1 THESSALONIANS 4:3

Terry Mattingly is a national columnist who often writes about how religion intersects with our culture. When he wants to know what a public figure or journalist really believes about Christianity and the Bible, he asks three questions:

1. Are biblical accounts of the resurrection of Jesus accurate? Did this event really happen?

2. Is salvation found through Jesus Christ alone?

3. Is sex outside of marriage a sin?

The first two questions are what you'd expect in a list like this. They go to the core of what a follower of Christ believes about our Savior. The third question is different. It goes to the core of what a person believes about Scripture and its role in a person's life today. If you really believe the Bible is God's Word, then you've got to come to grips with what it says about sex.

My guess is that most of you reading these words believe that Christ was resurrected and that salvation can be found in Him alone. But when it comes to whether sex outside of marriage is a sin, the gap between belief and faith may be enormous.

Sex is a subject what leads to the beliefs of our culture colliding head on with the truth of God's Word. This issue is a proving ground—a place where you really show how much you trust God, because He reserves this intimate and holy act for the marriage bed.

In the previous two devotions, we looked closely at Genesis 2:24: "Therefore a man shall leave his father and his mother and hold fast to his wife, and they shall become one flesh." In marriage you leave your parents, you cleave (hold fast) to your spouse, and then you "become one flesh." That term is one of the most beautiful and profound in Scripture. However, becoming one flesh involves much more than the physical act of intercourse—it is, in the words of Clifford and Joyce Penner, a "mystical union between husband and wife that unites two people as total persons . . . intellect, emotions, body, spirit, and will."[1]

The romantic, sexual love in marriage, says authors Gary and Betsey Ricucci, is part of . . .

> a mysterious experience of becoming one that is unique to biblical marriage. A husband and wife who stand before God in the covenant of marriage as sinners saved by grace possess the potential for a depth of intimacy that no other relationship can touch. It is an intimacy that clearly involves the physical, but much more as well—an intimacy of heart and mind, of spirit and vision, of faith and hope.[2]

The world tells us that it's prudish and old-fashioned to reserve sex for marriage. God's Word says marriage is the sanctuary God created for sex and only there, in the refuge of covenantal love, will you find sex at its best.

In fact, the very act of maintaining your purity is a key step in your growth as a follower of Christ. First Thessalonians 4:3-5 says, "For this is the will of God, your sanctification; that you abstain from sexual immorality; that each one of you know how to control his own body in holiness and honor, not in the passion of lust like the Gentiles who do not know God."

In the covenant of marriage two people become one, and they vow to forsake all others. If you think about it, one of the most important tests of your commitment will be in the sexual area—to flee from sexual immorality (see 1 Corinthians 6:18) and remain true to your spouse. The period before marriage is a time to build your faith muscles—to trust God when He says that He will not allow you to be tempted beyond your ability to endure it (see 1 Corinthians 10:13). When you remain pure, you strengthen your faith in God, and you strengthen your future spouse's faith in you.

Over the years I've heard many people say, "I wish somebody would have challenged us with these standards before we got married." But I've never heard anyone express regrets over remaining pure before marriage. Some couples wait until their wedding to kiss for the first time, and I applaud their strength and courage.

For those of you who are already having sex, the good news is that purity can be restored when you confess your sin and put your trust in Jesus to forgive you and restore your relationship with Him. The Bible promises, "If we confess our sins, He is faithful and just to forgive us our sins and to cleanse us from all unrighteousness" (1 John 1:9). God stands ready to forgive you, cleanse you and restore your purity the moment you ask.

I also want to challenge you to sign the purity pledge (p.61) as a commitment that you will abstain from sexual immorality until your wedding day. This will mean setting some strict standards about touching and about spending time alone. Avoid tempting situations. And go to a mature Christian who knows you both well and will hold

Purity Covenant [3]

Biblical Standard

For this is the will of God, your sanctification; that is, that you abstain from sexual immorality; that each of you know how to possess his own vessel in sanctification and honor, not in lustful passion, like the Gentiles who do not know God; and that no man transgress and defraud his brother in the matter because the Lord is the avenger in all these things, just as we also told you before and solemnly warned you. For God has not called us for the purpose of impurity, but in sanctification. So, he who rejects this is not rejecting man but the God who gives His Holy Spirit to you (1 Thessalonians 4:3-8, *NASB*).

In obedience to God's command, I promise to protect your sexual purity from this day until our wedding night.

Biblical Standard

Flee immorality. Every other sin that a man commits is outside the body, but the immoral man sins against his own body. Or do you not know that your body is a temple of the Holy Spirit who is in you, whom you have from God, and that you are not your own? For you have been bought with a price: therefore glorify God in your body (1 Corinthians 6:18-20, *NASB*).

Because I respect and honor you, I commit to building up the inner person of your heart rather than violating you.

Biblical Standard

In view of this, I also do my best to maintain always a blameless conscience both before God and before men (Acts 24:16, *NASB*).

I pledge to show my love for you in ways that allow both of us to maintain a clear conscience before God and each other.

This Is My Promise of Purity:

Signed: _____ Date: _____

Signed: _____ Date: _____

Witnessed/Affirmed by: _____ Date: _____

you accountable—someone who will regularly ask you, "Are you doing what is right? Are you being clean? Are you obeying God?"

This could be the greatest gift you could give each other. It's a clear statement of your intention to fulfill your vows and build a marriage of oneness that will last a lifetime.

Oh, and one other suggestion: Plan a short engagement!

1. Individually read through each section of the Purity Covenant.

2. After you have read through all three passages and the commitments, sign and date the covenant. Then have someone you know—pastor, counselor, friend or mentor—sign it as a witness.

Notes
1. Clifford and Joyce Penner, *The Gift of Sex: A Guide to Sexual Fulfillment* (Nashville, TN: W Publishing Group, 2003), p. 22
2. Gary and Betsy Ricucci, *Love That Lasts* (Wheaton, IL: Crossway Books, 2006), p. 116.
3. This Purity Covenant is adapted from FamilyLife's workbook for engaged couples, *Preparing for Marriage: Discover God's Plan for a Lifetime of Love,* published by Gospel Light.

13

The *Big* Day

BY BARBARA RAINEY

*Above all, keep loving one another earnestly, since love covers a multitude of
sins. Show hospitality to one another without grumbling. As each has received
a gift, use it to serve one another, as good stewards of God's varied grace.*
1 PETER 4:8-10

Whether your wedding is months, weeks or days away, one thing is
certain: You are in the middle of one of the most stressful periods of
your lives. Perhaps you've already learned that planning a wedding is
a breeding ground for tension . . . and conflict.

> Congratulations! We're so excited you're going to be part of
> our family! And guess what? The first thing we're going to do
> is work together to put on one of the biggest, most complex
> and most emotional events of our lives!

For most brides, the day they are to be wed is something they've
been dreaming about since they were little girls. Many have imagined
details that would astonish the groom—the dress, the flowers, the
colors, the music, the food.

For many parents, the day their child is to be wed is something
they've been anticipating for many years. For them it is a culmina-
tion of their parenting years—a celebration of God's provision of a

spouse for their child, an opportunity to rejoice in who their child has become, an occasion to mark a child becoming an independent adult. It's a momentous event for them, and they want to share it with family and friends.

Each family brings its own experiences and traditions into a wedding—its own sense of "normal" (more about the new normal in devotion 18). Sometimes all the differences mix easily, with little anxiety. But sometimes the differences are so great that problems and conflicts arise.

Maybe the groom's parents feel that too many people are being invited to the rehearsal dinner. Perhaps the bride and groom want a small, outdoor wedding, but her parents want a traditional church wedding with all their friends in the audience. Some grooms want to be very involved in all the details; some could not care less. Brides are no different, either gladly delegating the decisions and responsibilities or confidently writing the script and directing the entire cast of characters. In the worst scenarios, strong wills clash, and everyone involved becomes hurt and angry and eager for the whole thing to be over.

Two common mistakes visit every couple and their parents during the planning. First, in their eagerness and excitement they don't take time to consider everyone's perspective and expectations. Second, they don't think of the bigger meaning inherent in every wedding.

I thought the wedding is about us! It's our day, might be your first thought. And you would be right. But you would also be wrong. While you as a couple are the stars of the show, your supporting cast members need to feel valued, or hurt feelings will dampen everyone's enjoyment of the day.

A wedding is all about honor. God is honored for bringing you together and for creating the institution of marriage. You are honored as a couple as you occupy center stage. Parents are honored with front-row seating. Friends and family are honored with the privilege of being attendees, witnessing the celebration whether grand or simple.

Having been a bride who planned her own wedding and then the mother of the bride or groom four times, here are a few suggestions based on personal experience:

1. *Use this as an opportunity to build teamwork as a couple by talking about and listening to each other's desires and expectations for the wedding.* Listening is an important quality in marriage, so practice it now. Ask questions to understand the why behind each other's preferences on size of wedding and reception, budget, etc. (see also devotion 18).

   Talk about how you can honor God and family in your ceremony and reception. (For example, you might consider honoring your parents by writing them letters of gratitude, or a tribute as mentioned earlier, for what they've done well in raising you.) Decide what is most important to you and what you're willing to compromise on.

2. *Talk to and listen to all the parents involved.* Tell them that you want to do your best to understand their hopes and dreams and that you don't want to offend in any way. At the same time, let them know that, although you want everyone to be happy with the wedding, it's impossible for everyone to be happy about every decision.

   Saying up front that you want to include them goes a long way. Even if your wedding is next week, you can still say, "Thank you for all you have done up to this point. Is there anything we can add at this late date to make our day more like you've always imagined?" Or perhaps simply say, "Thanks for all you have done to make our wedding so wonderful. We hope you will enjoy it as much as we will."

Ultimately each parent is an individual who wants to be valued and appreciated and included. If your goal is to give each of them that value, your wedding will indeed be glorious.

3. *Give everyone involved the same grace that God gives to you.* As 1 Peter 4:8-10 tells us, we should love one another, serve one another and show hospitality without grumbling. When disagreements happen—and they will—be quick to apologize if you are at fault; if you're not at fault, give grace to those who are. There is always more going on behind the scenes than you realize.

Giving grace will be necessary for the rest of your life, so practicing it today is a good idea. The relationships you have with most of the people involved with your wedding will be waiting when you return from your honeymoon, so nurturing them well will pay dividends later.

∞ DISCUSS ∞

1. Matthew 5:9 says, "Blessed are the peacemakers, for they shall be called sons of God." What can you do between now and your wedding day to be peacemakers—to sow seeds of harmony between you and your families rather than discord?

2. It has been said, "Make the most of the best and the least of the worst." Talk about how you can encourage one another to do this as you go through all the preparation for The Big Day.

3. Pray together that your wedding day will honor God for how He brought you together. Pray that your families will also feel honored so that their joy is as great as yours.

14

About Your *Honeymoon*...

Count it all joy, my brothers, when you meet trials of various kinds, for you know that the testing of your faith produces steadfastness. And let steadfastness have its full effect, that you may be perfect and complete, lacking in nothing.
JAMES 1:2-4

Barbara and I have fond memories of our honeymoon. We began in Houston, staying at the Warwick Hotel. We dined and danced and were delighted as we glided silently in an elevator with a view of the skyline. Then we journeyed to the Rocky Mountains, where we stayed in a cabin on the White River, camped at 8,000 feet (we nearly froze), fished, explored and took pictures of the aspens in their fall glory. Although we've since traveled all over the world, that adventure remains one of our favorite experiences.

That's definitely not true for every honeymooning couple, however. After hearing several stories of "honeymoons gone bad," I've determined that ours couldn't have gone much better. I don't want to frighten you, but I do want to prepare you for the fact that honeymoon experiences often don't quite match expectations.

Everyone wants the perfect wedding and the perfect honeymoon, but real life has a way of editing human dreams and sometimes turning them into something, well, less than perfect. We asked our online readers to send us stories of bad honeymoon experiences, and they replied with some of the worst horror stories we've ever read.

Sickness was a common theme—stomach problems, migraine headaches and just plain exhaustion were common ailments suffered after the hectic days and weeks leading up to the wedding. One bride described how she woke up early on her wedding day with terrible stomach problems, fell back asleep and awoke only two hours before the ceremony. Then she was so weak that her father had to hold her up as they walked up the aisle. Two days later she was admitted to a hospital and had her gall bladder removed.

Then there was the wife who nearly ran over her husband with a boat while he was on a jet ski. Her boat did slice his foot open, and she was so upset that she could barely drive him to the hospital. "I didn't completely lose it," she wrote, "until we got to the hospital; and while he was being treated, I ended up on the gurney next to him, dry heaving, light headed, and dizzy. The doctor working on his 17 stitches assured my husband that I wouldn't be reacting this way if I didn't really love him."

There also was the groom who came down with three types of food poisoning during their honeymoon in Cancun. And the couple that fell asleep while soaking up the rays at a beach resort—and got so sunburned, they spent the next three days in their room, unable to wear clothing or do *anything*! Then there was the couple who went online to book a peaceful, secluded cabin, only to learn it was "smack-dab in the middle of a major chicken-farming area." Because of the cabin's location, the smell of chickens was pervasive: "The outside of the cabin smelled. The inside of it smelled. The smell was unmistakable and unavoidable."

Perhaps the most unusual story came from the couple who, at the end of their honeymoon, were depositing money at a bank that turned out was being robbed at the same time. (Apparently it was a quiet robbery!) Their car was mistakenly identified as the getaway vehicle, and police pulled them over as suspects. They were both handcuffed, and three officers aimed weapons at the young bride. They were eventually released when a witness cleared them.

I guess that these unfortunate couples learned very quickly that a honeymoon is often very different from what had been expected. Most of us would choose not to encounter trials like this during a honeymoon, but I found it interesting that many of these readers look back on their honeymoon horror stories as valuable lessons for their marriages. For example, the woman who had her gall bladder removed said she and her husband now realize it was "part of God's plan to help us cope with some of the trials that our marriage has gone through during the past 36 years, and to learn to trust in Him during these times."

James 1:2-4 tells us that we should "count it all joy" when we experience trials, because the testing of our faith produces steadfastness. And that's a character quality that we need to exhibit in marriage. This was abundantly clear to a woman who told the story of being stuck for hours at night on a Hawaiian road, waiting for a landslide to be cleared: At the time there was nothing positive or funny about the situation. However, today we are both able to look back and have a good laugh, as well as see that we were given a taste right off the bat to what real marriage would look like—roadblocks, rain and potential for blame. But we persevered and learned to tackle our problems together.

In addition to seeing God at work in your circumstances, use your honeymoon to begin to develop a good sense of humor about unmet expectations and unusual situations. Over your lifetime together, you'll need it! (Send your "epic" honeymoon story to my Facebook page or to Dennis-Rainey@familylife.com.)

✑ DISCUSS ✑

1. Read James 1:2-4 and Jeremiah 29:11-13. What do you learn about God in these passages?

2. How does God work in a person's life during times of suffering?

3. If you can, share about a time when you've seen God work for good in your life during a time of trial.

4. Pray together that God would give you the strength and wisdom to "count it all joy" and have the ability to see God at work in everything that happens during your honeymoon—the good and the bad.

15

Don't Be a *Grasshopper*

We are not able to go up against the people, for they are stronger than we are.
NUMBERS 13:31

I remember the first time I walked into the office of Bill Bright, while he was still president of Campus Crusade for Christ. As I looked on his desk and walls, I was fascinated to see what he valued. Of course, there were pictures of his wife and family, awards he'd received and mementos from around the world. But on his desk there was an engraved brass plate with the most unusual phrase I've ever seen in an executive office: "I'm no grasshopper."

I asked Bill what "I'm no grasshopper" meant. He chuckled and started telling me the Old Testament story about the Israelites returning to their homeland after centuries of slavery in Egypt. Their leader, Moses, sent 12 spies into the land of Canaan. The land was inhabited by "giants," but God said He would give it to the short guys, the Israelites.

Ten of the 12 came back and reported that it was impossible for the Israelites to conquer the land: "We are not able to go up against the people, for they are stronger than we are," they said. "We seemed to ourselves like grasshoppers, and so we seemed to them" (Numbers 13:31,33).

Only two of the spies, Caleb and Joshua, said the land could be taken. Joshua said there would be nothing to fear, because the people could trust in the Lord (see Numbers 14:8-9). But the people would not listen. As a result, the Israelites did not attempt to conquer the land God said He was giving them, and they spent 40 years wandering around in the wilderness because of their unbelief. They had become grasshoppers in their own minds.

After recounting this story, Bill turned to me and said, "Dennis, when I arrive in heaven, I don't want my life here on earth to have been characterized by viewing myself as a grasshopper. My God is so big, I want to expect and believe Him for great things."

I think of that story whenever I look at the challenges of this culture. The economy may go downhill, our moral condition may spiral downward, or our nation may be struck by terrorism; but I serve a big God. No matter what happens in my family or in my world, I don't want to become a grasshopper. I want to believe God for great things.

You face the same choice as you begin a new chapter of your life. If you haven't experienced hardship and suffering yet, you can be assured that you will during your years together. Will you respond to troubling circumstances like grasshoppers, or will you respond with trust in God, who is in control of your fate today just as He was in the days of Moses and Joshua?

You need to remember that *God is always in control,* even in times of uncertainty and moral chaos. Romans 8:28 is still true: "And we know that for those who love God all things work together for good, for those who are called according to His purpose." So is 1 Thessalonians 5:16-18: "Rejoice always, pray without ceasing, give thanks in all circumstances, for this is the will of God in Christ Jesus for you." I am also reminded of what Jesus said in the Sermon on the Mount:

> Therefore I tell you, do not be anxious about your life, what you will eat or what you will drink, nor about your body, what you will put on. Is not life more than food, and the body more

than clothing? Look at the birds of the air: they neither sow nor reap nor gather into barns, and yet your heavenly Father feeds them. Are you not of more value than they? And which of you by being anxious can add a single hour to his span of life? . . . But seek first the kingdom of God and his righteousness, and all these things will be added to you (Matthew 6:25-27,33).

These Scriptures tell two timeless truths that you need to focus on and embrace together as husband and wife

1. *God will provide for your needs.* His provision may come in different forms than you expect, but His promise to meet your needs has not expired in the twenty-first century. That's pretty important to remember in the early years of marriage, when you typically will not be earning as much money as you probably will in later years.

2. *There is more to life than meeting your daily material needs.* When you seek God's kingdom and His righteousness, you operate according to His priorities—you're concerned about building your family relationships and connecting the hearts of your children to God's heart. You are impacting future generations by proclaiming Christ, and thereby impacting your world for Christ. That's what life is really about.

Don't become a family of spiritual grasshoppers.

✑ DISCUSS ✑

1. Have you ever faced a challenge or a crisis of belief and forgotten who God is and what He promises—have you ever become a "grasshopper"? If so, share what happened. Now read Romans 8:28 again. In what ways have you seen the truth displayed that God is always in control?

2. Read the entire passage of Matthew 6:25-33. How have you seen God provide for you in times of need?

3. In what ways do you need to trust in God's control and provision right now as a couple?

4. Pray for one another that your future spouse will put his or her trust in God, regardless of the circumstances.

16

The *New* Normal

Love one another with brotherly affection.
Outdo one another in showing honor.
ROMANS 12:10

There I would be, snuggled in our warm bed, about to drift off to sleep. And then would come the dreaded question from my wife: "Honey, did you remember to turn out all the lights and lock all the doors?"

That was our story during the beginning of our first year of marriage. One night, though, Barbara's question took a dreadful turn. You have to understand that we lived in Boulder, Colorado, where the winter nights were cold, and we both loved our toasty electric blanket. I remember the night when I collapsed into bed, totally exhausted, and Barbara brought me back from the edge of oblivion with a light poke and a variation of the nightly question: "Aren't you going to turn out the lights?"

It occurred to me at that moment that for the past two months I'd been the one getting up and experiencing mild frostbite and that perhaps it was her turn. "Why don't *you* turn out the lights tonight?" I retorted.

Barbara replied, "I thought *you* would, because my dad always turned out the lights."

Whoa! A shot of adrenalin cleared my head like the sun piercing the fog. And I shouldn't have said it, but I did: "But I'm not your dad!"

Well, that turned out to be a night when we practiced the scriptural admonition to "not let the sun go down on your anger" (Ephesians 4:26). You see, two powerful forces clashed on that cold Rocky Mountain night—Barbara's sense of normal and my sense of normal. She felt it was the husband's duty to turn off the lights, because that's what her father had always done. That was normal to her. But in my family of origin, that task was not assigned irrevocably to the male of the species.

Each of you brings a different background and a different set of expectations into your marriage. Your family did things a certain way, and your spouse's family did things a certain way. Often you don't even realize what's normal to you until you get married, and suddenly you learn that your spouse's family did things differently.

For example, think about some of the normals surrounding your family and dinnertime:

- Was it normal for you to eat dinner as a family on most nights?
- What types of meals did you normally eat?
- What did you drink?
- Who cooked the meal?
- Who cleaned up?
- How did you normally dress?
- Did you open the meal with prayer?
- Did you start eating when you were seated or did you wait until after you prayed?
- Was it normal to get a debrief from everyone's day or was the television the center of attention?
- If someone called on the phone, would dinner be interrupted by the call being answered?
- Was it normal to have friends over for dinner?
- How often did you eat at restaurants as a family?

You could probably add to that list. And that's just one set of normals. How about breakfast and lunch? What were your normals regarding family entertainment? Vacations? Birthday celebrations? Christmas gifts? Pets? Handling finances?

In your relationship, you've probably already experienced a clash or two between your normals. And you will undoubtedly face collisions in the near future over these unspoken rules. In their book about the first year of marriage, Susan DeVries and Bobbie Wolgemuth write, "Over the years we've seen couples in conflict over money or sex or in-laws, but what they're really fighting about aren't those things at all. They're really fighting about *normal*."[1] That's why you should make it a priority early in your marriage to *create a new set of normals* in your relationship.

First, *commit to understanding each other's normals*. Make the normals of your future spouse part of your vocabulary. If you find yourself disagreeing about an issue, ask yourselves, "Is this a question of differing normals?" Create a spirit of discovery, where you can talk about normals in a way that doesn't feel threatening. Remember that in most cases different is not bad—it's just different.

Second, *make choices together that reflect your priorities and values*. Suppose you grew up in a family that gave each other inexpensive birthday gifts, while the family of your spouse-to-be splurged and spent a lot more money. As you consider how to celebrate your birthdays, this is an opportunity to make your own choices that reflect the importance you place on birthdays, and the number of banks you have to rob so you have enough to spend.

As you make these decisions, follow the guidance of Romans 12:10: "Give preference to one another in honor" (*NASB*). In most cases your sense of normal will not be superior to that of your spouse. If you both determine not to hold too tightly to what's comfortable and familiar, you will find ways to compromise and honor each other and create your own normal in your new home.

So . . . who's going to turn out the lights in your family?

∞ DISCUSS ∞

1. Think over conflicts you've experienced in your relationship. Can you trace any of them back to the underlying issue of what is normal to you?

2. Your wedding may be a good opportunity for you to practice establishing your own normal. Start by answering the following questions:

   • How are weddings normally celebrated in your church or community?
   • Who is usually invited to the rehearsal dinner? To the wedding?
   • What will be your family's expectations about the wedding reception?
   • What is normal for your family regarding the cost of the wedding?
   • In what ways are your normals different as you approach your wedding?

3. What's most important to you in the wedding? Now see if you can agree upon what is most important to both of you in your wedding. Write it down in a place where you will be reminded what you two agreed to.

4. Pray together, asking God to give you the wisdom to understand your different normals as your relationship grows and matures.

Note

1. Susan DeVries and Barbara J. Wolgemuth, *The Most Important Year in a Woman's Life* (Grand Rapids, MI: Zondervan, 2003), p. 44.

17

The *Very Best* Single Piece of Advice *I Can Give* You

*Therefore, confess your sins to one another and pray for one another,
that you may be healed. The prayer of a righteous person
has great power as it is working.*
JAMES 5:16

When I was a newlywed in 1972, I asked my boss and mentor, Carl Wilson, for his single best piece of marital advice. He and his wife, Sarah Jo, had been married 25 years.

"That's easy," he said. "Pray together every day. Every night for 25 years we have prayed together as a couple."

Since that day several decades ago, Barbara and I have rarely missed daily prayer. This discipline has helped resolve conflicts, kept communication flowing and, most importantly, acknowledged our dependence upon Jesus Christ as the Lord and builder of our marriage and family.

I am not certain that Barbara and I would still be married had it not been for the spiritual discipline of experiencing God together in our marriage. It has kept us from building walls in our marriage, it has encouraged us to build bridges by forgiving one another, and it has kept us focused and traveling in the same direction.

DENNIS & BARBARA RAINEY

So I say with confidence that *if there is one simple spiritual discipline that I would passionately challenge couples to begin adopting in their marriages, it is this one: the habit of praying together every day.*

I remember one night when Barbara and I ended up in bed, facing opposite directions after an argument. I didn't want to pray with her that night. In my conscience, however, Jesus Christ was asking me, "Are you going to pray with her?"

"I don't like her tonight, Lord," I replied.

"I know you don't," He said. "But you're the one who tells people that you pray with your wife every day."

My response? "But Lord, you know that in this situation she is 90 percent wrong!"

To which He responded, "But it's your 10 percent that caused her to be 90 percent wrong!"

And I retorted, "Now, God, don't mess with the facts!"

Slowly, the Lord turned me over, and I said, "Sweetheart, will you forgive me for being 10 percent wrong?" No, just kidding! I apologized and asked Barbara to forgive me. She did. And Barbara and I talked and then prayed.

I thank God for that tradition of prayer He helped us build early in our marriage. I am not exaggerating when I say that Barbara and I might not still be married had it not been for daily prayer. You cannot invite almighty God into your marriage day after day and still be the same person. Where He shows up, He transforms things.

Surveys at our Weekend to Remember marriage getaways indicate that less than 8 percent of all couples pray together on a regular basis. And after interacting with tens of thousands of married couples at these events, I suspect that less than 5 percent of all Christian couples pray together daily.

We need to bring back a popular slogan from the 1950s: "The family that prays together stays together." I believe that if every Christian couple would pray together regularly, our nation would experience a spiritual renewal of historical proportions, including a dramatic drop in the Christian community's divorce rate.

I want to challenge you to begin praying together daily before you are married. Build the discipline into your daily routine now, and then continue it after the wedding.

Please don't say you're too busy for this. Saying you don't have time is not a statement of fact, but a statement of value. Don't let surfing the Internet, pursuing a hobby, working late, watching TV or any other busyness keep you from praying together. It's easy to get busy—we all have a lot going on in our lives. But don't get so busy that you can't make the time to pray together.

This may take some courage to implement. I've seen that look of hesitation and even fear in the eyes of many men when I've given them this challenge. It's way out of their comfort zone. But if you think about it, working through this devotional is already putting you on the right track. You're talking about your faith in God and about your relationship; and, I hope, you are closing each devotion with prayer.

When you pray together, you experience intimacy with Almighty God and one another. During the rugged times of your marriage, you can share your burdens. Prayer can also take away the desire to get even and replace it with a willingness to work things out.

I urge you to make a commitment to pray together every day. Make the commitment now. Like so many others, you may be afraid to start, but I can promise you that praying together will be one of the most rewarding things you will ever do for your marriage and for your family. And if you miss a day praying together, pick it up tomorrow.

✑ DISCUSS ✑

1. Have you found that praying together is easy or difficult? Why?

2. If you have not been praying together, what has kept you from doing this?

3. How have you seen God answer your prayers together as a couple?

4. Ask each other what you can pray for the other. Then hold hands and pray for each other. Also pray that God will give you the determination and perseverance to make this a daily part of your life together.

18

A *Marriage* with *No Hope*

(PART 1)

By wisdom a house is built, and by understanding it is established.
PROVERBS 24:3

If a house is built by wisdom, the flip side is also true: By foolishness a house is destroyed. Foolishness can create a lot of chaos in a marriage.

The marriage of Hans and Star Molegraaf is a living witness to the truth of how wisdom and foolishness affect a house—and to the grace of God. The Molegraafs' marriage is now built on wisdom, but at one time it was nearly destroyed by foolishness.

As Hans admits, "Star and I didn't know anything about marriage when we got started." He was 20 and she was 19. "Alcohol and sex were really a foundational part of our relationship," Hans says. "I wouldn't even say that we were really in love. I just think we were having fun together, and we were more infatuated with each other."

But when Star learned she was pregnant, they decided to get married. Their friends couldn't believe it. "They could see the alcohol, the yelling, the screaming and the fighting—there was, already, physical abuse in our relationship . . . It was almost comical to them that we were going to do this."

Sure enough, it didn't take long for their marriage to sour. They loved their new daughter, Kylie, but they knew nothing about building a marriage relationship.

One of the big problems was that Hans could not control his anger. He would grow frustrated during an argument because Star could outtalk him. At first, all he would do was yell and scream; but he began to go further, grabbing Star and shaking her, or throwing her onto the bed. Then he'd fall on his knees, beg her forgiveness and swear it would never happen again. But then it did happen again. Repeatedly.

Star had grown up watching her stepfather become physical with her mother, and she had always feared her marriage would be the same. And now it was. "It was my worst fear coming true," she recalls. "It was happening right before my eyes, and I felt like it was moving so fast that there was really nothing I could do to stop it."

Star begged Hans to go to counseling with her, but he wasn't interested. Eventually, seeing no future for their marriage, Star moved in with her mother, taking Kylie with her. She also began an affair.

When Hans asked his parents if he could stay with them, they agreed on one condition: "If you are going to live in our house," they said, "we want you to go to marriage counseling."

"Dad, you don't understand," Hans said. "Star doesn't want to have anything to do with me. She is just not going to go."

"No, *you* don't understand," his dad replied. "I want you to go by yourself."

So that's how Hans reluctantly ended up in a counselor's office. In his mind, Star was at fault. He began the session by listing her faults: She didn't love him as she should. She didn't respect him. Didn't the Bible say a wife should respect her husband?

In response, the counselor read from Philippians 2:

> Count others more significant than yourselves. . . . Have this mind among yourselves, which is yours in Christ Jesus, who,

though he was in the form of God, did not count equality with God a thing to be grasped, but emptied himself, by taking the form of a servant, being born in the likeness of men. And being found in human form, he humbled himself by becoming obedient to the point of death, even death on a cross (Philippians 2:3,5-8).

When Jesus Christ came to earth, the counselor told Hans, He deserved for people to worship Him. But He came with the attitude of a servant, putting others before Himself.

This was the turning point for Hans—and also for his marriage that had almost been destroyed by foolishness. It was the moment when God stepped in and changed him. "When I compared my life with how Christ Jesus lived His life, my sin was exposed," he says. "There was some type of spiritual transformation that happened in that moment."

Hans had gone into the counseling session, focusing on how Star had failed him. He left the session "broken at how I had contributed to our issues in our marriage."

You may never face the same type of problems in your marriage relationship as Hans and Star. They were young, immature and ill-prepared for marriage. But I am confident that, at some point, you will come to the same turning point Hans did: At some point you will need to decide whether to keep on blaming your spouse for your problems or whether to accept responsibility for your contributions to the house you have built.

Proverbs 29:1 says, "He who is often reproved, yet stiffens his neck, will suddenly be broken beyond healing." Will you be proud, or will you be broken over your sin?

∽ Discuss ∽

1. Read Philippians 2:1-11. What does "count others more significant than yourselves" (v. 3) and to look "also to the interests of others" (v. 4) mean? What do you think that looks like for you in marriage?

2. How can you apply in your relationship the truths found in Philippians 2:1-11?

3. Pray together, asking God to give you the humility to confess your sins to one another and to regard each other as more significant than yourselves.

19

A *Marriage* with *No Hope*

(PART 2)

If the Spirit of him who raised Jesus from the dead dwells in you, he who raised Christ Jesus from the dead will also give life to your mortal bodies through his Spirit who dwells in you.

ROMANS 8:11

In the previous devotion we began the story of Hans and Star Molegraff, a couple seemingly without hope in their marriage. But one thing we've seen countless times over our lifetime is that nothing is hopeless when Jesus Christ shows up. If Christ can overcome death, He can defeat any problem you two are facing.

After Hans was confronted with his sin while meeting with a counselor, his life began to change. And Star didn't know how to respond. She was enjoying her new life separate from Hans, and she was dating another man. But she couldn't help noticing the transformation in Hans. "He was becoming the man I always dreamed he would be, but there was such severe brokenness in our relationship that I wasn't certain I could ever have an intimate relationship with him again."

Surely, Star thought, *this change wasn't real.* She tried to provoke Hans's anger, anticipating he would respond as he had in the past. She

DENNIS & BARBARA RAINEY

wanted everyone to see he had not changed. "I can remember throwing everything that he had ever done into his face. . . . He would just say, 'I know. I know. I am so sorry.'"

Star decided to see the same counselor that Hans was meeting with, figuring it was a necessary step toward getting the divorce she wanted. "I vented to him everything that Hans had ever done to me and just every reason why there was no way this could work." Her thinking was, *Certainly God would not want me in a marriage where I am miserable.*

Finally the counselor said, "Star, I need to ask you something."

"Okay, what?"

"I need to ask you if you believe that Jesus Christ was raised from the dead."

"Yes, I believe that."

"You don't hear what I am asking you," the counselor said. "Do you believe it? Do you believe that God took that dead man out of the grave, raised Him to life so that He could save you?"

"Yes! I believe that."

"You think God can take a dead man—raise Him to life again to save you—*but you don't think that same God can heal your marriage?*"

That was the moment everything changed. "Part of my heart was opened up in a way that it had never been opened up before," she recalls. "I remember wondering, *What if God could do it? What if He could give me what I had always wanted in our marriage?*"

Hans and Star began to connect with each other—love each other, enjoy each other. She confessed her affair and was astonished to see Hans forgive her instead of exploding in jealousy and anger. "I realized that she is responsible for her actions, but in my mind, I really saw it as my fault," Hans explains. "I had seen the way that I had treated her for the first 18 months of our marriage. I didn't blame her for having an affair. I was not a loveable man."

Hans was applying the truth of Ephesians 4:32, which commands: "Be kind to one another, tenderhearted, forgiving one another, as God in Christ forgave you." As Hans says, "How could I have not forgiven her? In this stage of my life, my sin was so exposed in my life, and I saw and was receiving God's forgiveness for everything that I had done. . . . How could I not give that same forgiveness away?"

From that point on, Hans and Star were, in Hans's words, "on fire for the Lord" and "on fire for each other." They went through counseling together, and they attended a Weekend to Remember marriage getaway sponsored by FamilyLife. "It totally blew me away that God really had a plan for marriage," Star says, "that we could do it His way and that it could work—that I didn't just have to survive—that I didn't just have to stay with this man because it was the right thing to do but that we could have something beautiful."

Hans and Star were part of a group of friends from high school who all married at about the same time. Today they are the only couple of the group still married. A marriage without hope—a marriage that, humanly speaking, should have broken apart—is thriving because two people turned from their selfishness and believed that God could work in their lives and resurrect their marriage. Two broken people surrendered to Christ.

If God has the power to raise His Son from the dead, is there any problem in your life and in your relationship that He cannot heal?

✑ DISCUSS ✑

1. Read Romans 8:9-11. What does this passage tell you about the power God gives you through Christ?

2. Think back over the time you have known each other and dated. What are some examples of God giving you the wisdom and power to address different issues in your relationship?

3. Identify a problem you are facing right now—individually or as a couple—that needs the same power that raised Jesus Christ from the dead. How can you pray about this problem?

4. Pray for one another and the issue(s) you are facing. Pray that you will both be open to God's work in your lives. Pray together that the God who raised Christ from the dead will give you power through the Holy Spirit and enable you to be wise in knowing what to do when troubles come.

20

Who Is Your Closest Neighbor?

For the whole law is fulfilled in one word:
"You shall love your neighbor as yourself."
GALATIANS 5:14

Lamar was an angry man. Not violent, just angry—and bitter.

His children had grown rebellious. He had been through back surgery and two hip replacements; then he lost his job and went on disability. He grew angry at God and decided he wanted out of his marriage. "I don't love you. I don't need you. I don't want you," he told his wife, June.

June wouldn't give him a divorce, so he said, "Well, just leave me alone." He didn't move out, but he stopped talking to her. Totally.

For the next *three years* Lamar and June continued living in the same home as husband and wife, but they didn't speak. June continued serving her husband as she had before—cooking for him, cleaning his clothes, mowing the yard.

June's parents and her grown children urged her to get a divorce. "God doesn't want you to suffer like this," they said. But she felt that God wanted her to stick with her husband. In the silence, she spent more time reading the Scriptures and praying. In her journal one day she wrote, "Lord, I cannot change this man, but You can change me."

Eventually, faced with such determined love, Lamar was bound to crack. He broke his silence and told June that he didn't know if he could love her again, but he wanted to restore their marriage. "And it wasn't two weeks before he was calling me darling and telling me he loved me," she says. Their marriage settled into a new pattern of selfless love. "It was almost like we were in a contest to see who was going to outdo the other."

This story admittedly describes an extreme example of a marriage in trouble, but it is one of the best stories of selfless love we've seen. June determined to love her spouse no matter what he did. And her faithfulness had a huge impact on the children who had once urged her to get a divorce. Now they tell her, "We don't want to miss out on what God has to teach us, even during the hard times."

Matthew 22:35-41 records a remarkable statement by Jesus Christ:

> And one of them, a lawyer, asked him a question to test him. "Teacher, which is the great commandment in the Law?" And he said to him, "You shall love the Lord your God with all your heart and with all your soul and with all your mind. This is the great and first commandment. And a second is like it: You shall love your neighbor as yourself. On these two commandments depend all the Law and the Prophets."

In other words, you could sum up the entire Bible in these two commandments. The first addresses how you should relate to God, and the second, "love your neighbor as yourself," how you should relate to other people.

Now consider this: Who is your closest neighbor?

Your spouse.

Treating your spouse as your closest neighbor is more than being selfless—treating your spouse as more important than yourself, as you are instructed in Philippians 2:1-8. Rather, it is an active love that seeks opportunities to please and serve and encourage, even when your spouse is not doing the same in return.

So what does "love your spouse as you love yourself" mean?

One way of finding an answer in Scripture is to look at the "one another" passages. These talk about encouraging one another, building one another up, confessing your sins to one another. One of these passages is Colossians 3:12-14:

> Put on then, as God's chosen ones, holy and beloved, compassionate hearts, kindness, humility, meekness, and patience, bearing with one another and, if one has a complaint against another, forgiving each other; as the Lord has forgiven you, so you also must forgive. And above all these put on love, which binds everything together in perfect harmony.

Do you want your spouse-to-be to show you kindness and compassion? Then that's what you should show to your future spouse. Does it please you when your future spouse bears with you and forgives you when he or she has a complaint against you? Then you should do the same with your spouse-to-be.

Consider what good could happen in your marriage if you learned how to love each other the way you love yourself. Think of the intimacy and oneness you will enjoy. Think of the conflicts you will avoid as well as the conflicts you will resolve. All you need to do is apply this one simple and difficult commandment.

❧ DISCUSS ❧

1. Read the following "one another" Scriptures together and make a list of all the practical ways you can show love for your closest neighbor: Galatians 6:2; Ephesians 4:25; 5:19; Colossians 3:16; 1 Thessalonians 5:11; James 5:16.

2. Look over the list and tell your spouse-to-be about a specific instance when he or she has shown this type of love for you.

3. Create a short list of 3-5 ways your spouse can demonstrate love to you. Share your lists and discuss why each item listed is important to you.

4. Pray together for the ability to love each other as you do yourselves and to do this from the beginning of your marriage.

21

Marriage Secrets from the Real *Experts*

Gray hair is a crown of glory; it is gained in a righteous life.
PROVERBS 16:31

It's always good to learn from others who have experienced things before us. When you want to purchase a new computer or television, for example, you can go online and read reviews of the items that interest you. In the same way, you can learn from the wisdom of those who are truly "golden" and have built marriages that have lasted 50 years or more. Get a cup of coffee or tea and listen to some sage counsel:

> "Bill and I have learned that God has a plan for our lives, and when we realize that He's in control of all circumstances, it has a calming effect."

> "You need to have an attitude that you're going to be committed to marriage no matter what it takes. I'm just a firm believer that you have to be committed to marriage and to each other.
> And if you both love Christ and are conscientious about your conduct, knowing that you will have to give an account to Christ, I think that makes a huge difference in a person's life."

"In marriage you learn that God uses crooked sticks to draw straight lines!"

"God has used the hard times in our lives to draw us closer to Him and to help us depend on Him."

"If a husband is willing to come to his wife and ask for forgiveness, she should forgive him. Of course it might stay with her for a while, but after a while it won't worry her any more. When you forgive somebody you have to let it go. We have to forgive each other because God forgave us."

"Just have faith in the Lord and pray. Couples that pray together stay together. We rely on the Scripture: 'Trust in the Lord with all your heart and lean not on your own understanding. In all your ways acknowledge Him and He will direct your paths.'"

When I read quotes like these, two themes usually run through them. The first is that many of these couples—married at a time when divorce was not nearly as common as it is today—considered marriage a covenant, a lifetime commitment. Period. No escape hatches. No prenuptial agreements. No bail-out clauses. There were "in it to win it!" As one couple said, "We don't think of ourselves as being special. I don't feel like I'm special and don't think Glen does either. We got married and we're just supposed to stay married."

The other theme is the necessity of a strong commitment to Christ when working through the inevitable struggles of a lifelong relationship. Paul and Mona Sproull, for example, had been married 58 years when they were interviewed. But when they first married, Mona recalled, "We didn't realize that we were two very sinful people who needed a Savior."

One of Paul's problems from the outset was that he didn't know how to show affection. Even when he became a Christian a few months after they were married, he had trouble loving Mona with a Christ-like love. She told him, "I don't know how you can love God when you don't even know how to love me."

Four years later, she says she was "loaded down with a weight of sin and never felt rested." Then she saw a road sign that said, "Are you tired of living in sin?"

"My, oh, my, was I tired," she recalled. "Too tired for a 24-year-old. I stopped the car and cried my way through to His grace. Life changed for us at that time."

But they still faced many rocky years in their marriage relationship. Mona said, "Now that we are old, . . . we see how we hindered the Spirit for a lot of years when we didn't go to church and take God seriously."

Paul added, "For the first 31 years of our marriage, I had one of the world's worst tempers. I ruined automobile transmissions, broke equipment and doors—all out of anger. In 1979 I asked Christ to take complete control of my life and got deliverance from my temper, alcohol, cigarettes, you name it. . . . I am so grateful."

Even during the difficult years, the Sproulls clung to their marriage, and in their twilight years they were enjoying the benefits. "Today, Mona and I think about love in a far different vernacular than most people," Paul said, "We think of each other as the greatest things since Pepsi Cola, and there's no place in our marriage for anything but total commitment to one another and to God."

❧ DISCUSS ❧

Special project: This little assignment could be one of the biggest payoffs in this book. You are about to embark on the journey of a lifetime—marriage—and you can benefit from the wisdom of couples who are have traveled to the other end of the road. Find two or three couples in your family or church who have been married 40 years or more. Ask if you can bring dinner (maybe a pizza, but ask first) to their house and have them share their stories with you. Devise your own Top 10 List of questions, but be sure to include these three:

1. What have been some of the struggles you've faced in your marriage, and how did you work through them?

2. What would you advise a couple not to do if they want to stay married?

3. What's the best piece of advice you could give us as we begin our marriage?

Of all the things you are told to do in this book, this little assignment could have the biggest payoff, so take it seriously

22

You *Have* the *Power*

Perfect love casts out fear.
1 JOHN 4:18

I recall the day that I asked Barbara why she had not disciplined one of our children for what appeared to be a clear instance of disobedience. I was surprised when she replied that she wasn't confident of her judgment. "You're a great mom," I told her. "And your batting average is far better then you are giving yourself credit for. Trust your judgment and decide—God will lead you. And I have confidence in you!"

Later Barbara told me that she needed my encouragement—it showed that I believed in her, even when she didn't believe in herself.

We all need the love and encouragement of friends, family and mentors; but there's nothing like the support of a spouse. You may not realize it yet, but nobody else will have as much power to build you up as your spouse will have—not even your parents.

This is something Barbara and I learned early in our marriage. I will never forget what a surprise it was for me as a young man, a new husband, to realize that my wife had serious questions about herself, that she had self-doubt. She needed me to believe in her, to help her, to point her to Christ as her sufficiency. And Barbara discovered how much I needed her to help me become the man God was calling me to be.

You have a special power in the life of the person who is about to become your spouse. And there are two ways you can express this power when you are married:

First, *love and accept your spouse-to-be unconditionally.* True intimacy in marriage is risky. We all fear rejection, and in marriage it's common to think, *If you really knew me, you wouldn't accept me. If you really knew what I am like on the inside—who I am as a person—you would reject me. You might not love me anymore.* So the more you are transparent in your marriage—freely sharing your deepest thoughts and emotions—the more vulnerable you feel. Is it any wonder that a divorce is so traumatic? The person who knows you the best has rejected you.

It is powerful to know that the one who knows you best loves you the most—that your future spouse accepts you and loves you in spite of all your faults. As 1 John 4:18 says, "Perfect love casts out fear."

Accepting your future spouse and loving him or her unconditionally means continually remembering that he or she is God's gift to you. It means giving him or her the freedom to fail and when failure happens, offering forgiveness. It means making your home a safe place where your spouse knows he or she can be him- or herself without condemnation. It means loving your spouse as Christ loves the Church.

Second, *look for ways to build up your future spouse.* This does not mean controlling or manipulating your spouse-to-be to meet your standards or specifications. But you do have a special power in your relationship to encourage and help your future spouse walk more closely with God and become the man or woman God desires.

Does your spouse-to-be get discouraged? Be a cheerleader who will accept every failure, celebrate each victory and provide gentle encouragement to press forward and be courageous. One thing Barbara has done for me over the years is remind me of the truth about who I am: I am God's man. She reminds me of what God has done for me, for us as a couple and for us as a family. This is especially helpful when I'm feeling doubtful or discouraged or lacking confidence as I'm facing a tough situation.

Does your future spouse have difficulty making decisions? You can come alongside and help build his or her self-confidence. Coach and encourage your future spouse in how to think through choices; point out good decisions made in the past; help analyze poor decisions so that lessons can be learned from them.

Does your spouse-to-be have potential that needs to be nurtured? Many of us barely know what we do well at the time we're married. Become a student of your future spouse. What are his or her unique gifts and abilities? At what does he or she excel? What do you see your spouse-to-be doing that he or she really enjoys. Expand your future spouse's borders—to try something dreamed about but never before given permission to try.

In recent years I've encouraged Barbara to pursue her interest and skill in art, and it's been a delight to see how she has blossomed. It's even turned into an outreach as she has begun developing beautiful resources to help families know and apply the Scriptures and bring meaning to holidays.

God has indeed given you a special power in the life of your future spouse. The question is, How will you use it?

✑ DISCUSS ✑

1. What are two or three ways that your future spouse demonstrates love and acceptance to you?

2. What are some areas where you feel you are growing as a result of your relationship?

3. Pray together that you would wisely use the power you have in each other's life.

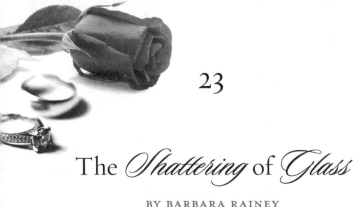

23

The *Shattering* of *Glass*

BY BARBARA RAINEY

You have made my heart beat faster with a single glance of your eyes.
SONG OF SOLOMON 4:9, *NASB*

It was the perfect setting for romance. We were in Mazatlan, Mexico, with some friends. We had a nice dinner and even danced. The weather was warm, and when we returned to our beautiful hotel room, a soft breeze was blowing off the beach into our room. We could hear a band playing music. It felt like a scene from a movie—all the ingredients were there for romance . . .

And then it all collapsed with angry words, tears . . . and shattered glass.

Let me set the stage a little more clearly. This trip to Mazatlan came at the end of a period that we now call our first season of suffering. All of the following happened within a 12-month period:

- We were cheated out of several thousand dollars in the purchase of a home.
- We faced medical issues with our 18-month-old child.
- We experienced financial stress, because we didn't have enough funds raised for our ministry.
- My father-in-law died suddenly of a heart attack.

- In the middle of winter Dennis suddenly had to run his family's business when his brother suffered an apparent heart attack, and then Dennis suffered from an anxiety attack and ended up in the same hospital as his brother.
- I collapsed one morning when my heart began racing at three hundred beats per minute, and Dennis rushed me to the hospital. (This was the first of several episodes over the next few years, until my condition was addressed with surgery.)

At the end of that yearlong storm, we felt like strangers. Romance was at an all-time low. So we were grateful when some friends offered to take us to Mazatlan for a much-needed getaway. We found someone to take care of our two young children, and we began a trip that we thought would rekindle the romance.

Things didn't turn out that way.

We were still young, still learning about our emotions and about our romantic needs as a man and a woman. As we returned to our hotel room that first night, Dennis was in high gear—he was ready to connect physically. After the storm we had experienced over the last year, he was ready to switch from the weather channel to the romance channel. But I was stuck back on the weather channel: I needed to talk and process again what I was feeling about our lives. I needed to feel closer emotionally before I could respond sexually. So when he began to initiate making love, I just couldn't respond.

And Dennis, in his frustration, took a bottle of hand lotion and threw it across the room, where it shattered a pane of glass. Of course the breakage had been unintentional, but was I shocked! And he was just as surprised.

Perhaps it took that shock to alert us to the fact that we still had a lot to learn about marriage. We both came face to face with our selfishness and with the different expressions of our needs. We are both broken people, and we need Jesus to work in our lives and to make our marriage what He wants it to be. We can't do it on our own.

That moment of crisis also brought us a new understanding of how different we are as man and woman. We were both addressing the same need, which is intimacy in a marriage, but we were coming at it from opposite directions. Our blow-up helped Dennis understand that I could not switch channels like he could—that I needed to talk and connect emotionally before we enjoyed physical intimacy. And it helped me learn to pay more attention to my husband's need for sexual affirmation.

As you begin your marriage, remember that your sexual relationship will do more than bind your hearts and souls together as you become "one flesh" (Genesis 2:24). It also will act as a thermometer of your relationship as a whole. If a marriage is going through a rocky spell or if a spouse is struggling with an emotionally difficult issue, the problems will almost always manifest themselves in the sexual relationship. That was certainly true in our relationship. For sex to be truly satisfying for both partners, each has to be totally open and vulnerable to the other. Each person must feel needed, wanted, accepted and loved sacrificially.

✑ DISCUSS ✑

1. From your observations, in what ways do men and women view romance and sex differently?
2. It's possible that during your honeymoon you may experience some pressures like I describe in my story. It's very common for couples to arrive at a honeymoon destination totally exhausted physically and emotionally. Then they become frustrated because their sexual intimacy does not come as easily as they had anticipated. Pray together that God will help you understand each other's needs in this area as you begin your marriage.

24

Emotional Adultery

But among you there must not be even a hint of sexual immorality.
EPHESIANS 5:3 (*NIV*)

High school chemistry taught me a very valuable lesson: When certain substances come into close contact, they form a chemical reaction. I proved that during my senior year of high school when I dropped a jar full of pure sodium off a bridge into a river and nearly blew up the bridge!

What I've learned since then is that many people don't respect the laws of chemistry any more than I did as a teenager. They mix volatile ingredients without giving much thought to the consequences. I've discovered that many people also don't understand that a chemical reaction can occur with someone other than their spouse.

Don't misunderstand me—I'm not just talking about sexual attraction. I'm referring to a reaction of two hearts, the chemistry of two souls. When you are married and you begin talking with someone of the opposite sex about intimate struggles, doubts or feelings, you may be sharing your soul in a way that God intended exclusively for the marriage relationship. This is emotional adultery—an intimacy with the opposite sex outside of marriage, an unfaithfulness of the heart. Emotional adultery is friendship with the opposite sex that has progressed too far.

This can be a difficult subject for engaged couples to grasp. You probably can't imagine becoming emotionally entangled with anyone else. But it's important to understand how easily this can happen and to take some precautions to protect your marriage relationship, starting even before your wedding day. Take note of the following actions that could result in emotional adultery:

- Communicating with another person that you have a need that you feel your intended isn't meeting—a need for attention, approval or affection
- Finding it easier to unwind with someone other than your future spouse by dissecting the day's difficulties over lunch, coffee or a ride home or through email correspondence
- Beginning to talk with someone other than your spouse-to-be about problems you're having with your intended
- Rationalizing the "rightness" of a relationship with someone else by saying that surely it must be God's will to talk openly and honestly with a fellow Christian
- Looking forward to being with someone other than your future spouse
- Wondering what you'd do if you didn't have this friend to talk with
- Hiding from your intended a relationship you have with another person

Connecting with another person as a substitute for your future spouse will be the beginning of your travel down a road that veers off too often into the ditches of adultery and divorce. So how do you protect yourself to keep this from occurring?

First, *know your boundaries.* Put fences around your heart to protect sacred ground reserved only for your spouse, and start putting up the fences now. Barbara and I are careful to share our deepest feelings, needs and difficulties only with each other.

For some, this may mean gracefully and tactfully pulling back on some friendships with the opposite sex. Perhaps you have a good friend who has been a sounding board and encouragement for years. The problem is that this relationship has changed now that you've committed yourself to marriage. That type of transparency should be reserved only for your intended.

Second, *realize the power of your eyes.* Your eyes are indeed the windows to your soul. Pull the shades down if you sense someone is pausing a little too long in front of your windows. I realize that good eye contact is necessary for effective conversation, but there's a deep type of look that must be reserved only for your future spouse.

Frankly, I don't trust myself. Some women may think I'm insecure because I don't hold eye contact very long, but I don't trust my sinful nature. I've seen what has happened to others, and I know it could happen to me.

Finally, *never stop courting your spouse-to-be after you are married.* One of the most liberating thoughts I've ever had in my marriage relationship is that I will never stop competing for Barbara's love. As a result of that commitment, I work at being creative in how I communicate with her relationally, emotionally, spiritually and sexually.

I am well aware that if I start taking her for granted, someone else could walk into her life and catch her at a weak point. My constant goal is to deepen our relationship and let her know that she is still the woman I decided to carry off to the castle in 1972.

Many people who commit adultery express surprise that it happened; they talk as if they were carried along by an irresistible force of nature. But remember that nobody who stands 40 feet away from the edge falls off a cliff. The danger comes when a person inches closer and closer to the precipice. Make your relationship such a priority that you don't come anywhere near the edge.

∽ DISCUSS ∽

1. Read Ephesians 5:1-3. How can you apply the truths in this passage to your relationship?

2. What are some boundaries you could set in order to prevent yourself from slipping into emotional adultery with someone of the opposite sex—so that "not . . . even a hint of sexual immorality" is present in your life?

3. Discuss how you would handle the situation if your spouse told you that another person was flirting with him or her. How about if your future spouse felt uncomfortable with a particular relationship with someone of the opposite sex? Would you be a "safe" person for him or her to share what's taking place?

4. Pray together that God would give you the commitment to reserve emotional intimacy for your marriage. If one or both of you have a friendship that needs to be adjusted because you are now engaged, pray that you will have the sensitivity and wisdom to make the adjustment in a way that your friend understands, and supports the change.

25

Setting Up *Guardrails*

The prudent sees danger and hides himself,
but the simple go on and suffer for it.
PROVERBS 27:12

I was attending a Christian writer's conference and staying at a hotel that had the world's slowest elevator, so I decided to use the stairs. As I stepped into the stairwell, I looked down and there it was—a pornographic magazine with a centerfold pulled out for all to see. It was like a trap . . . set just for me!

It's amazing how quickly the mind works. In a millisecond, my thoughts went from *Wow! I can pick it up and put it in my briefcase—no one will ever know,* to, *God will know,* to, *I'll have to tell Barbara.* I forced my eyes away from the gravitational pull of the magazine, stepped over it and walked down the stairs.

More than 12 hours later I used the stairs again to return to my room. Sure enough, there was the magazine. If it had been a bear trap with its jaws gaping at me, it wouldn't have been any less real. Once again I stepped over it and went on up to my room.

We all face temptations on a regular basis. But now, several years after the incident in the stairway, I look back on the episode as an important step in my life, my marriage, my family and, ultimately, my life's work. Someone has said, "The doors of opportunity swing on the little hinges of obedience." Had I caved in, who knows all that may have been wrapped up in that temptation?

The experience also helped me understand the need for guardrails in my life. On a highway, guardrails prevent me from driving too close to something dangerous—a cliff, a lake or oncoming traffic. In my personal life, a guardrail is a self-imposed rule that I set to protect myself and my marriage.

For example, I've set a rule that I will not meet with another woman alone in a closed room or in a restaurant. I also will not travel alone in a car with any woman other than Barbara. Am I being over the top? Perhaps, but over the past four decades these guardrails have protected me and helped me keep my distance from other women, and they help me avoid the appearance of evil.

Guardrails like these can be inconvenient, but I like the perspective Jerry B. Jenkins mentioned while he was interviewed on our radio program, *FamilyLife Today*. Jerry wrote a book on this topic called *Hedges: Loving Your Marriage Enough to Protect It*, and he has in place several hedges for himself. For example, if he's traveling somewhere to speak and the event organizer mentions that a woman will pick him up at the airport, he replies, "Well, I have a policy where if a woman comes to pick me up, have somebody else there, too, or send a guy." This may cause some awkward moments on the phone, but Jerry says, "I will trade that embarrassment for 34-and-a-half years of marriage any day."

Some of the most important guardrails concern the eyes. Luke 11:34 tells us, "Your eye is the lamp of your body. When your eye is healthy, your whole body is full of light, but when it is bad, your body is full of darkness." I may not be able to avoid that first glance at a pornographic magazine lying in a stairwell, a suggestive image in a television commercial or even a seductive-looking woman walking through the mall. But I can keep my eyes from lingering. I can look away.

Guardrails are important for wives too. Early in our marriage I led a small group of men that met at our home. After the group had met a couple of times, Barbara came to me and told me she was uncomfortable with one of the men, because he was acting too friendly and flirtatious. She said she was tempted to not tell me, but by telling me she disarmed what could have become dangerous. I moved the meetings to a restaurant.

Guardrails help keep you accountable to one another. They promote security, safety and trust in your relationship. They tell the world, "My marriage is my top priority." And they pronounce a declaration to your intended spouse, "I *will* protect our relationship."

∽ DISCUSS ∽

1. Read Proverbs 27:12. How does this verse tie in to the subject of setting guardrails in your life?

2. Share with one another some of the most common temptations you face. How could these affect your marriage relationship? Discuss how you could help protect one another from giving in to these temptations.

3. What are some guardrails you could set to help protect you and your relationship now and for the future?

4. Pray that God will give you the perception to recognize temptations and dangerous situations when they come, to be honest about them and to be wise in dealing with them. Pray also for the strength to honor and protect your relationship with each other now and in the future.

26

The *Shadow* of the *Past*

For all have sinned and fall short of the glory of God.
ROMANS 3:23

A young man came to me for counsel before he was married. He was 32, and he was still a virgin. But his fiancée had just confessed to him that she had had a sexual relationship with a man in the past, before she had become a Christian. So this young man was struggling—he had saved himself, had prayed for God to give him a wife, and now he was about to marry a woman who would not be able to offer him the same gift he had saved for her.

As we talked, it was interesting to hear him freely admit how God had forgiven him many times over the years for a variety of issues. He didn't deny his past transgressions. But because of the importance of the sexual union, his fiancée's transgression was a difficult issue for him to settle, and I could understand that.

You know what he did? He chose to forgive her, love her and receive her as God's gift to him. He married her. And it's important to note that she chose to receive him in *his* fallen state as well. His being "pure" in one area didn't mean that he wasn't tarnished in other areas.

Marriage is the union of two broken, selfish and sinful people. And isn't that true of all of us? "All [of us] have sinned and fall short of the glory of God" (Romans 3:23). That's why marriage is such a beautiful picture of Christ's relationship with the Church—we choose to forgive each other, receive each other and commit to love one another just as God did with us through Christ.

All of us are influenced by what has happened in the past. We've all made some good choices and some bad ones. And though we are new creatures in Christ, we still carry the scars of our sins in the past—they influence how we act and how we treat one another.

The past eventually pushes to the surface in a relationship; it won't stay hidden. Remember, you are about to pledge to give everything you are—past, present and future—to your future spouse. However, there may be some issues from your past that you are ashamed about or embarrassed by, and you may be afraid to admit them to your spouse-to-be. Yet if you don't, you will always wonder, *If he really knew me, would he still love me?* These secrets can threaten your relationship. And you will miss out on the real power and majesty of what God wants you to experience in your marriage.

Here are a few principles to remember when dealing with past sin experiences:

1. *The truth needs to come out now.* If past sins emerge after you are married, the revelation might create feelings of betrayal. And it might destroy the trust you need to sustain your marriage.

   For example, suppose that one of your past sins was immorality. Imagine what would happen to your relationship if, after the marriage, a visit to a doctor revealed that you had a sexually transmitted disease—and that your spouse now had the disease (you'd be surprised at how often this happens).

   Or what if you have had problems with handling money, with alcohol or drugs, or with pornography? What if you've been involved with an abortion? To the best of your ability, you need to admit these failures now, not later.

This doesn't mean you should confess all the morbid details, especially in regard to sexual matters (those images don't need to be crashing around in your intended's mind). But hiding the issues will lead to bigger problems in the future.

2. *Dealing with the past gives you the opportunity to experience the beauty of forgiveness.* Remember, forgiveness is the heart of Christianity and the heart of marriage. You are two imperfect sinners who will become one in marriage, and you will be pledging to express continually God's love and compassion and forgiveness to each other. That is a beautiful thing! It's what marriage is about, and you will forgive over and over and over again.

Frankly, if before you get married you cannot forgive each other as Christ has forgiven you, you should not get married. It's that simple. If you can't exercise forgiveness now, what guarantee can you give that you will be able to exercise it later? Being unwilling to forgive is a deal breaker.

3. *"Perfect love casts out fear"* (1 John 4:18). The past can tear down a person. It can wound the soul. But unconditional love in a marriage is a healing force. It says, "I embrace you, I receive you, I accept you. You are God's gift to me, no matter what has happened in the past, and no matter what I will learn in the future."

There will still be surprises in the future. The shadow of past experiences will affect you in ways that you cannot predict. But revealing past sins now provides a wonderful place for a marriage to start—a place of grace, forgiveness, love and total commitment.

Remember: To forgive others means you give up the right to punish them. If you struggle with forgiving your future spouse because of some past failure or indiscretion, we encourage you to get alone with God and work through forgiving him or her *before* you get married.

Reflect: Both of you should take some time to prayerfully consider your past and evaluate if there are issues that need to be shared with your future spouse. Ask God for wisdom to determine if a third party (pastor, counselor, or a godly advisor) needs to help in the process of communicating these issues.

∽ DISCUSS ∽

1. Read Romans 8:38-39. If nothing can separate you from the love of Christ, what should your attitude be about your future spouse's past?

2. Read 1 John 4:18. Why is it true that "whoever fears has not been perfected in love"? In what ways have you experienced love from your future spouse that "casts out fear"?

3. Before praying together, read 1 John 1:9-10, then pray together thanking God for His grace and forgiveness in your lives. Pray that you will not condemn yourself for sins that have been forgiven, and pray that you will not condemn your future spouse for the same.

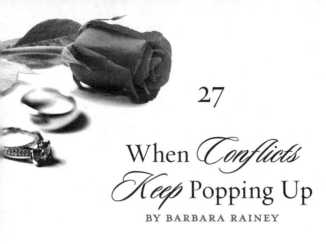

27

When *Conflicts* *Keep* Popping Up

BY BARBARA RAINEY

When I am afraid, I put my trust in you. In God,
whose word I praise, in God I trust.
PSALM 56:3-4

Perhaps you've played the Whack a Mole game—it's found at many kids' pizza parlors. The machine pops up plastic moles, and your mission is to beat them back down as fast as they come up. You will learn that conflicts in marriage are like that game; they keep popping up in new places, no matter how hard you work to get rid of them.

Recently, Dennis and I were in another unwanted skirmish over an old issue in our marriage. Same topic, same emotions, round gazillion! I once thought that we should be able to resolve cleanly and permanently all our issues, but I've learned that's not the case. Some issues are not black and white, so they repeatedly pop up.

Over the years of our marriage, our repeated disagreements fit into several categories: parenting values, decision making, money, sex and travel. Our most recent conflict was the old "we're traveling too much" issue.

Before we were married, Dennis's mother affectionately called her son a roadrunner, after the cute cartoon character that is always getting away from the coyote. I thought it was sweet. However, I should have paid attention to what she was really implying by that name! It wouldn't have changed my decision to marry him. But his roadrunner-like enthusiasm for travel, adventure, discovery, and conquering enemy territory has caused more ongoing stress and conflict in our marriage than any other issue.

The "we're traveling too much" conflict began when I realized we were over-committed. Again. Somehow the schedule monster had eaten up more days than we realized, and we suddenly found ourselves facing the enemy of miscommunication with no escape. I prefer to spend more time at home than Dennis does; Dennis needs me to go with him, support him and do life with him. Neither of us is wrong. Our perspectives are just different. It's what we do with the clash of those colossal differences that matters.

At the core of this recurring conflict is my fear that I am not really valued for what is important to me. If I perceive that Dennis is constantly scheduling us to the brink, pushing me to my limits, then I conclude he hasn't heard me, doesn't get it and, therefore, doesn't love me. At the same time, if I refuse to adapt, to grow, to risk the stress of following him, then he perceives that I haven't heard what he needs, I don't get it and, therefore, I don't really care about him as a person.

Each time we clash over this issue, we peel away another layer of the "onion." Each conversation strips off our individual coverings so that we can see ourselves and each other more clearly than we did before. In this conversation, for example, we realized that I need margins in my schedule for different reasons than I did 20 years ago when I was parenting full time, and Dennis now needs my partnership for different reasons, too.

Each time this issue pops up in our relationship, we learn more about each other, and we also return to two critical keys of resolving conflict:

1. We need to discuss our differences with teachable hearts, willingness to change and openness to admit wrong thinking, attitudes and behavior.

2. We need to pray together and trust God through every circumstance and every problem in our relationship.

Our perceptions of ourselves and each other are vastly flawed. We often forget how our selfishness affects how we view our conflicts. In this latest disagreement I saw more clearly than ever before that I need to work on my attitude about following my husband, that I need to rejoice that my husband wants me with him and that I should trust God with this situation that He has given me for my good.

During a recent snowstorm, our office building closed. Dennis and I decided to enjoy every minute of the glittering snow-covered day, so we donned our winter gear and went hiking in the woods. On the way back I paused to catch my breath from an uphill climb. As we stood there panting, he said to me, "I'm not going to push you anymore." He was talking about the hike, not the travel issue, but I realized in that promise that he had heard me. He allowed me to be who I was in that moment—needing a pause in the action when he didn't.

∽ DISCUSS ∽

1. What have been some repeated disagreements you've already faced during your relationship (maybe over finances, in-laws or wedding plans)?
2. Read Psalm 18:2 and Psalm 56:3-4. What do you learn about God in these verses?
3. Why is it important to maintain your complete trust in God while you're experiencing conflicts?
4. Spend some time talking about a conflict or disagreement you're facing now. Talk about being heard, being teachable and being willing to change. How are you doing with these qualities?
5. Pray together that God, through His Spirit, would give each of you a heart of humility and trust in Him.

28

Frequent *Forgiveness*

BY BARBARA RAINEY

Be kind to one another, tenderhearted, forgiving one another,
as God in Christ forgave you.
EPHESIANS 4:32

I know that many aspects about marriage are different from what I expected, but one of the biggest surprises to me has been that, although we've been together since 1972, our need to forgive each other is as fresh as it was on our wedding day. You'd think we would have learned not to say unkind things, not to hurt each other, not to take each other for granted.

But we are imperfect human beings who don't love each other as well as we wish. Henri Nouwen wrote, "Forgiveness is love practiced among people who love poorly." And because we love poorly, we must forgive frequently.

Sometimes I wish that wasn't the case—that we would outgrow the need to forgive each other frequently. But then I remember that this is what Christianity is all about.

The Bible is the story of a loving and compassionate God pursuing His stubborn, sinful creation. He demonstrated this love by sending His Son, Jesus Christ, to die for us while we were still sinners (see Romans 5:8). He forgave us and made it possible for us to enjoy fellowship with Him. And He calls us to forgive each other as Christ forgave us (see

Ephesians 4:32). That's why marriage is a reflection of the gospel—a picture of Christ's relationship with the Church.

Christianity, then, is all about forgiveness. And a great marriage, in the words of Ruth Bell Graham, is "the union of two forgivers." Two imperfect people living together will need to forgive each other multiple times—maybe even each day. And by the way, if you add children to the family, the need for forgiveness will be compounded, because of the number of sinful people who are living under one roof!

One of my favorite stories about forgiveness is that of Joseph in the Old Testament. He was sold into slavery by his jealous brothers, who told their father that he had been killed by a wild animal. In Egypt, where Joseph was taken, he was again, this time to an officer in the army. Later he was unfairly sent to prison for something he did not do. But instead of being angry, Joseph believed God was with him. He believed God was to be trusted, feared and obeyed.

Eventually, through God's providence, Joseph rose to a position of great power and influence. Fast forward another 12 years, and Joseph was busy meeting with people from all over the world who had come to request food to survive a severe famine. And who showed up begging for food? His brothers.

Joseph could have used his power to seek revenge on his brothers, and who would have blamed him? Instead he forgave them and told them, "Do not fear, for am I in the place of God? As for you, you meant evil against me, but God meant it for good, to bring it about that many people should be kept alive, as they are today" (Genesis 50:19-20).

Joseph's story illustrates the truth that *forgiveness means giving up the right to punish the person who sins against you.* Often it may feel as if you are going against everything inside you—your desire for justice, for revenge. But it is grace in action—giving the person something he or she doesn't deserve.

Perhaps that's why forgiveness will feel more reasonable, and perhaps a bit easier, if you remember the grace of God in your own life.

The power of forgiveness lies in its ability to replay God's forgiveness over and over. Forgiveness announces the gospel and its unparalleled healing power to a broken world.

In the end, forgiveness means cooperating with God's plan. Joseph recognized that God had directed His life for His own purposes: God had taken an unspeakably cruel act that Joseph's brothers had meant for evil and, ultimately, had used it to save the Jewish people.

In a similar manner, you must cooperate with God's plan for the intimate relationship you share in marriage. Your spouse may hurt you more deeply than any other person ever has. Yet if God forgives you daily, how can you not do the same?

∾ DISCUSS ∾

1. What does it mean to forgive each other "as God in Christ forgave you" (Ephesians 4:32)? Individually write down a list of things for which Christ has forgiven you. Then share your lists.

2. Why is forgiveness difficult in a relationship? How much has forgiveness been part of your relationship?

3. Share with each other one or two situations where it was difficult for you to forgive another person.

4. Pray together, asking God to give you hearts of compassion, humility and forgiveness. Ask Him for the strength to forgive each other as He has forgiven you.

29

The Grand Illusion

*For the love of money is a root of all sorts of evil, and some
by longing for it have wandered away from the faith.*
1 TIMOTHY 6:10, *NASB*

Your marriage will be susceptible to the American Dream Syndrome.
Through an endless parade of messages in this media-driven culture,
you are sold the notion that you can *have it all* and, what's more, that
you *deserve* to have it all, sooner rather than later.

It's easy to be seduced by the grand illusion of the American Dream
Syndrome. After all, advertisers parade before your wide-open eyes a
colorful host of gadgets, toys, cars, home furnishings as well as every
imaginable convenience.

What goals do advertisers hope to achieve? To make you discontent with what you have. To infect you with "affluenza" and a *desire
to acquire*. They want you to want to live large now—in many cases,
just like your parents do. They want you to want to own a big house,
drive the cool cars, use cutting-edge technology, send your kids to the
best schools, join expensive clubs and take that extended cruise. And
as you already know, there's a legion of credit cards to assist you in
fulfilling your every desire.

And don't underestimate the role of peer pressure in the spread of
the American Dream Syndrome. The lifestyle choices you see made by
your families, friends and neighbors can put you in a truly amazing
race to have all the latest gear.

Over the years, I've identified three myths of the American Dream Syndrome:

- Myth #1: Getting stuff will make a person happy.
- Myth #2: Having lots of stuff is a sign of personal significance.
- Myth #3: The person with the most toys wins.

These myths influence you more than you want to admit because they tempt you to live beyond your means. And that's a major reason why handling finances is often such a struggle in a marriage—particularly for newlyweds. In this culture it is absolutely essential to go into marriage with a biblical view of finances and a shared determination to take control of your spending.

Larry Burkett, who was an expert on money matters, once said, "Of the couples who end up getting a divorce, every survey shows between 85 [and] 90 percent of them say that the number one problem they were having was finances." This means that the decisions you make about budgets, debt and what you value as a couple will be among the most important decisions you make as you begin your life together. And I believe there are five key steps you both must take to start off on the right track.

First, *embrace God's perspective of money by studying what the Bible says about money*. The Scriptures make it clear, for example, that God is the real owner of all that we have, and we are stewards of the resources God has entrusted to us. These truths should first influence your attitude about money. For example, you should not take pride in the money you make, because it really all comes from God. He is the One who providentially provides it to whom He pleases. As Psalm 50:10 tells us, "For every beast of the forest is mine, the cattle on a thousand hills."

Scripture also calls us to avoid giving our devotion to money. Ecclesiastes 5:10 says, "He who loves money will not be satisfied with money, nor he who loves wealth with his income."

Second, *commit together to put God, rather than money, at the center of your life.* Married couples who struggle financially often have their allegiance in the wrong place. Jesus said, "No one can serve two masters, for either he will hate the one and love the other, or he will be devoted to the one and despise the other. You cannot serve God and money" (Matthew 6:24). Jesus knew that the desire for money could be so great that we would pursue it instead of pursue a closer relationship with Him.

Third, *commit to being content with what you have.* Solomon wrote, "Again, I saw vanity under the sun: one person who has no other; either son or brother, yet there is no end to all his toil, and his eyes are never satisfied with riches" (Ecclesiastes 4:7-8). If you are discontent with what you have, you will never reach the point of having enough, because enough will never be enough.

Contentment arises from a spirit of gratefulness and thankfulness. It is a courageous and contagious choice to thank God for what you have *and* for what you don't have.

If you want to avoid the trap of the American Dream Syndrome, learn to be content with your portion by practicing a life of thankfulness. The apostle Paul wrote, "Give thanks in all circumstances; for this is the will of God in Christ Jesus for you" (1 Thessalonians 5:18).

Fourth, *adopt a team approach to handling your finances.* At the most basic level, this means talking together regularly about your money. Don't make anything off limits, and remember that it's okay to disagree. Early on, agree on a monthly budget and live by it, plan a strategy for saving and investing, and give to the church and to God's work. Oneness in your approach to handling finances is not an option. Work through what you value and your differences.

Finally, *commit to stay free of consumer debt.* Falling for the grand illusion of the American Dream Syndrome leads directly to suffocating credit card debt for far too many couples.

In fact, if you face a large amount of consumer debt right now—before your marriage—you should consider postponing the wedding until you erase it. This may sound harsh, but the fact is that you've already got a track record of handling finances poorly, and those habits won't change after the wedding. Seek the counsel of your pastor or some trusted Christian friends or mentors on this issue. Establish a plan to pay off all debts.

Remember that material things will never fill the void in your soul. They will never satisfy the hunger in your heart. In fact, that hunger will grow and grow. The more you acquire, the less satisfied you will be. Why? Because only Jesus can satisfy that void.

A couple who fails to see this could spend a *lifetime* chasing the American Dream, only to find it's like a desert mirage—forever just out of reach. One of the wealthiest businessmen in America, John D. Rockefeller, was once asked, "How much money do you need to make?" To which he replied, "Just one more dollar than I have."

∾ DISCUSS ∾

1. There are about 2,000 passages in the Bible about money. Why do you think God's Word addresses this subject so often?

2. Read Proverbs 22:7; Malachi 3:10; Acts 20:35; Philippians 4:19; 1 Timothy 6:10. How can you apply these passages to your finances—how you think about money and how you handle it?

3. Do you have a budget that you both have agreed upon? What steps do you need to take together to get control of your finances before your wedding?

4. Pray together that God would give you the wisdom to make good decisions about your finances and the courage to take difficult steps to assume control of what God has entrusted you with.

30

What About *Children?*

Behold, children are a heritage from the Lord,
the fruit of the womb a reward.
PSALM 127:3

Right now you are focused on the life you are about to begin together. But for a few moments, let's gaze into the future. Where do you see yourself 10 years from now? What do you hope to be doing? What do you want your marriage to look like? How would you describe your family? How many children would you like to have?

Your picture of the future may be a little fuzzy when it comes to children, because you're focused on the wedding. I know that's how I was when Barbara and I were engaged. When I was a single man, I don't recall even *liking* children. I don't recall even having a thought about the number of children I'd like to have. Children were not on my radar screen.

But after Barbara and I married and we celebrated our second anniversary with our newborn daughter, Ashley, *everything* changed. God performed heart surgery on us—we truly began to understand the blessing children bring. And God continued to bless us with a full house of these gifts. Then we understood another truth that Solomon wrote about children: "Blessed is the man who fills his quiver with them" (Psalm 127:5). Once you become involved in the process of loving these gifts and connecting your heart to theirs, you realize that becoming a parent truly is one of God's greatest rewards.

DENNIS & BARBARA RAINEY

Have you discussed having children with your future spouse? You really should have a talk about this before you marry. And there are two basic questions you should face as you talk about having children: (1) When will you start? and (2) How many would you like to have? Swirling around these basic questions are a dizzying array of related questions involving individual issues regarding such things as health, family backgrounds, priorities and use of contraception (or not). Right now the most important thing you need to grasp is God's heart for children, because I've found that many couples are unaware of what God says in the Bible on this subject.

1. *God commands us to "be fruitful."* Genesis 1:28 records that after creating man and woman, God commanded them, "Be fruitful and multiply, and fill the earth." This concerned more than the obvious need to add to the human race. It also was a timeless command—a declaration that bearing and raising children is part of God's plan for a husband and wife.

   I realize, of course, that there are couples who face issues such as infertility or health problems and are unable to have children. In those cases, adoption should be prayerfully considered. In that way the scriptural standard for a marriage to produce offspring can still be fulfilled.

2. *Children are a blessing, not a burden.* Psalm 127:3-5 tells us that every child is "a heritage" from God, "a reward," and we are "blessed" by having them. "This is different from the world's schizophrenic perspective about children. On one hand, children are celebrated in our culture: Parents express their love and devotion to their kids; and the media portray families and children in heartwarming stories. On the other hand, children are also regarded as a burden:

They are expensive, they interrupt careers, they require an amazing amount of sacrifice, they get on nerves, they interfere with plans, etc.

It's true that you may not always regard children as a blessing; and as Barbara once pointed out to me, "You know, people today need to be warned that having children will cost you." But as we talked about all of the joys and challenges of raising six children, we concluded that we could not imagine life without them. Raising them was one of the highest and holiest privileges we've ever been given.

In fact, at the end of our conversation I said, "If I had it to do all over again, I think I would want *more* children!" Barbara wholeheartedly agreed.

3. *Families are a central part of God's plan for spreading the truth about God and the experience of God from generation to generation.* Psalm 78:5-8 and Deuteronomy 6:4-8 make it very clear that parents are expected to implant God's truth into the lives of their children . . . who will then pass it on to their own children . . . who will then pass it on to their own children and so on and so on. God's original plan called for the home to be a greenhouse—a nurturing center—where children grow up to learn character, values and integrity.

Children are the spiritual messengers that we send with the gospel to future generations. Children are our legacy and a vital part of God's plan for us in marriage.

∽ DISCUSS ∽

1. As you look to the future right now, when do you anticipate having children? How many would you like to have? Answer these two questions individually, and then share them with each other. Talk about any fears and the reasons behind your answers (for example, if you anticipate waiting five years before you have children, tell your reasons for waiting).

2. How does your own family background influence your answers to these questions?

3. Read through all the Scriptures mentioned in this devotion. In what ways does God's view of children figure into your plans?

4. Pray together, asking God to enlarge your hearts for children, to bless your marriage with children, to give you wisdom in raising them and to make you of one heart and mind as you support each other as parents.

31

You're Joining
a *Family*

If possible, so far as it depends on you, live peaceably with all.
ROMANS 12:18

I wish I knew how to relate to my mother-in-law. Sometimes we get along wonderfully, and she seems like a real friend. And at other times she treats me like I'm a child. Last week we had dinner at their house, and she was ordering me around and correcting me like I was a servant. She wants to be in charge, and gets angry if I don't do what she wants. Does she forget that I'm an adult now, with a family and home of my own?

Those words echo the feelings of countless young husbands and wives as they learn how to relate to their in-laws. But I left one thing out: The man who uttered these words has been married for over 25 years. "I never dreamed that I'd still be dealing with these same issues after all these years," he says. This man's dilemma illustrates a simple truth about marriage that seems to elude many people when they get married.

When you get married, you make a commitment to love your spouse "until death do you part," right?

Right.

Do you understand that this means you're also making a commitment to your spouse's family?

Of course.

And that they will be part of your lives for 30, 40, 50 years—"until death do you part"?

Really? That long?

You aren't just marrying your spouse. You're joining a family—with its own traditions and eccentricities and patterns of belief and behavior. You will be part of their lives, part of their history that is being written each day and each month.

You may be spending holidays with them for the rest of your life. You may join them for vacations, family dinners, birthdays, anniversaries, weddings and funerals. Those in-laws who think you aren't good enough to marry their child? In 30 years you may be helping make decisions about whether those in-laws can continue living on their own.

I hope that you will find that joining a new family is a rich experience. But it's very likely that you will, at least occasionally, also find it challenging, beginning with the days that lead up to your wedding.

The Scriptures don't specifically address how to survive a three-day family reunion with your in-laws and extended family. But take a look at the advice on relationships in 1 Peter 3:8-12 and see if it doesn't seem written with in-laws in mind:

> Finally, all of you, have unity of mind, sympathy, brotherly love, a tender heart, and a humble mind. Do not repay evil for evil or reviling for reviling, but on the contrary, bless, for to this you were called, that you may obtain a blessing. For "Whoever desires to love life and see good days, let him keep his tongue from evil and his lips from speaking deceit; let him turn away from evil and do good; let him seek peace and pursue it. For the eyes of the Lord are on the righteous, and

his ears are open to their prayer. But the face of the Lord is against those who do evil."

It's one thing to apply this passage to relationships with neighbors, coworkers or friends. But it may be more difficult to apply it to new family members, because you (and they) live life up close and personal. You all see the good, the bad and, no doubt, the ugly in each other. But this passage may still be your survival guide if you keep these points in mind:

1. *Maintain an attitude of sympathy, brotherly love, tenderness and humility.* As a couple, be the ones in your family who consistently demonstrate the love of Christ. There will likely be a person or two in your spouse's family that will be your "irregular" person—a person difficult to love and get along with. Make up your mind to allow the Holy Spirit to love that person through you; and express toward that person tenderness, humility and, as needed, compassion.

2. *Return a blessing for evil.* What are you going to do when your mother-in-law intentionally hurts you or insults you, repeatedly? The natural impulse is to seek revenge, but Scripture calls you instead to forgive her and to do something that may be even more challenging than forgiving: to go on the offensive and to bless her by being kind to her, serving her, or by finding ways to encourage her.

3. *Keep your tongue from evil.* Fight against the temptation to play the game of one-upmanship. It serves no real purpose if when your in-laws are critical of you, you are even more critical of them behind their backs or possibly even to their faces.

4. *Be a peacemaker, not a troublemaker.* Don't allow bitterness to grow in your heart. Seek to resolve conflicts quickly. Fulfill Romans 12:18: "If possible, so far as it depends on you, live peaceably with all." That may not be truly possible to be in total peace, but as much as it depends upon you, seek to be at peace with your in-laws.

There will be much in your new family that you cannot control. Decide to look at your situation this way: As you grow in wisdom and spiritual maturity and consistently demonstrate the love of Christ, you can become a force for good in your new family. No matter what they believe about Christ, they will have the opportunity to see Him working in you. You may never see their attitudes change toward God or you, but you will have done what is right in God's eyes.

∽ DISCUSS ∽

1. How would you describe your current relationship with your future in-laws? What have been the benefits of getting to know them? What have been the challenges?
2. Read 1 Peter 3:8-12 again. What are some specific ways you can apply these truths as you relate to the different people in your new family? Be specific and name the person and what action you need to emphasize.
3. Pray together that God would help you to understand your in-laws and where they come from in life. Pray that He will work through you to love your in-laws in such a way that they would see Christ in you.

32

If *Only* We'd *Known* ...

*I do not cease to give thanks for you ... that the God of our Lord Jesus Christ,
the Father of glory, may give you the Spirit of wisdom and of revelation in the
knowledge of him, having the eyes of your hearts enlightened.*

EPHESIANS 1:16-18

I suppose there are some things we only learn by experience. But I do
wish someone had told me—before my wedding—about what I was
getting into.

To be honest, I was an idiot during my first year of marriage. I repeatedly ignored the dignity of the woman God had given me. I didn't
understand our differences, and I focused on my needs rather than
hers. I failed to love her in so many ways.

I wish I had known how self-centered I could be. Here I was, a
follower of Christ, committed to being part of fulfilling His Great
Commission (see Matthew 28:18-20), and yet I was surprised by the
level of selfishness that I displayed as we adjusted to living with
each other.

People are stubborn, and sometimes we only learn things the
hard way, through experience. But there are many traps that couples
commonly fall into during the early marriage years, and sometimes a
timely word of advice can help couples avoid them. We recently asked
readers of *FamilyLife*'s website, "What do you wish you had known
before you were married?" Their responses were fascinating:

DENNIS & BARBARA RAINEY

"I wish I had known how to resolve conflict without saying the wrong things or hitting below the belt."

"Your spouse has secrets."

"Healing takes time."

"Marriage does not mean you get to have sex anytime you want it."

"Marriage is a full time job . . . it must be always tended like a fire in the fireplace so that it will keep burning well."

"Forget perfect."

"I wish I had known how to forgive generously and quickly."

"The person you love the most is also the person who can hurt you the deepest."

"Never stop improving your commitment to your spouse and your marriage."

"You can't change your spouse, only God can."

Two themes appeared most often in the responses.

The first theme is that doing *marriage right is difficult*—more than you think it will be when you're engaged. "Marriage is work!" one reader wrote. "Marriage is compromise and sacrifice. It can end in happily ever after, but not without a lot of heartache and tears in between."

Another said, "I wish I had known how much work marriage was going to be, so I wouldn't have approached it so casually." I find it interesting that on one level we know intellectually that marriage will be difficult—otherwise, the divorce rate would not be so high—but on the other hand, we think it won't be hard *for us.*

The second theme is tied to the first: Because marriage is difficult, *you can't make marriage work in your own power.* To make your marriage last for a lifetime, you need to rely on God for the power, love, strength, wisdom, guidance and endurance you need. As one reader wrote, "Your marriage is not a one and one commitment, it is a *one and one and One* covenant between you, your spouse and God. Remember to keep Him first and foremost and He will help you weather the storms of life."

These responses echo the stories we've heard for years from our Weekend to Remember marriage getaways. It's not enough to know biblical principles about marriage and relationships. To build the type of marriage and family that you long for, you need to surrender your life to Christ and follow Him.

That's the lesson Brian and Julie Moreau learned after more than a decade of marriage. They saw no hope for their future because their relationship was marked by continual communication problems, money issues and an affair. They were headed for a divorce when some friends intervened and urged them to attend a Weekend to Remember getaway.

During that weekend, the Moreaus began to understand what they were doing wrong in marriage, and they felt hope when they heard about God's plan. When a speaker explained how to know Christ as their Savior and Lord, both Brian and Julie responded. And since that weekend they have not been the same. As Brian explained, "The bottom line was we both accepted Jesus and we now had that Helper [the Holy Spirit] to help us."

You will hear many words of advice as you approach your wedding day—and much of it may be on the theme of "what we wish we had known." And in this book we've given you more "what we wish we had knowns" to think about. But if you remember only one thing, I hope it is this: In the end, the success of your marriage will rest on whether you put God and the Scriptures at the center of your lives and your relationship.

∽ DISCUSS ∽

1. Go to your parents and the most mature married friends you know and ask them, "What do you wish you had known before you were married?"

2. Read Ephesians 1:16-20. Would you say that the eyes of your hearts have been enlightened so that you understand what knowing Christ means? Do you understand how to appropriate the "surpassing greatness of His power toward us who believe" as you approach your wedding day and begin to build your marriage? Do you have a relationship with God? (If there are any questions in your mind about how you stand with God, read the appendix, "The Secret to Building a Great Marriage and Family.")

3. Pray together that your marriage would be centered on God and your relationship with Him.

33

What *Robs* Men of *Courage?*

(FOR THE HUSBAND-TO-BE)*

Be strong and courageous. Do not be frightened, and do not be dismayed, for the Lord your God is with you wherever you go.
JOSHUA 1:9

In 2003, Hurricane Isabel slammed into the East Coast of the United States, first lashing North Carolina and Virginia and then moving northward all the way to Canada, leaving 16 dead and cutting power to six million homes.

The edges of the hurricane passed through Washington, DC, prompting the president and members of Congress to find safer quarters. That was not the case at Arlington National Cemetery, where guards have relentlessly stood vigil at the Tomb of the Unknowns every hour of every day since July 1, 1937. When the hurricane hit, the soldier on duty at the time remained at his post, even though he had been given permission to seek shelter.

Like that soldier, a husband is called to stand and do his duty while staring down the very storms that seek to rob him of courage, taunting and tempting him to neglect his duty and abandon his post as a man. And the storms a man faces pack as much (if not more) power than Hurricane Isabel did:

DENNIS & BARBARA RAINEY

Storm Number One: Damnable Training by Fathers

I once met a man who grew up in a remote section of our country. He admitted that the only advice he received as a boy from his father regarding women was, "Get 'em young. Treat 'em rough. Tell 'em nothing."

I wonder how that advice worked for him in his marriage.

You could say this is a legacy of the "strong, silent, tough man" image often passed down from father to son. This is the type of misguided training in manhood that has corrupted so many men as the leaders in their homes—selfish, repressive men who control their wives and children so that their own needs are met.

And that's just one part of the problem. Many boys grow up with fathers who are distant and passive. Fathers who rarely engage their families, and when they do, their half-hearted attempts to train their sons may promote irresponsible, or even immoral, behavior.

Too many men today were raised by fathers who didn't step up to their responsibilities. Is it any wonder we have a generation of men who feel lost and aimless, not knowing how to face their fears or think rightly about themselves, women, and their own passions?

Storm Number Two: Fatherless Families

The relentless, ruthless winds of a culture of divorce have uprooted the family tree, and with it at least two generations of men. With our high divorce rates and the increasing number of births to single women, the number of children in the United States who live in a single-parent household has more than doubled since 1978.

Children are the innocent victims of this raging storm. The bottom line: Dad is AWOL in far too many homes today.

One of the greatest challenges any boy could endure is trying to become a man without a father to show him how. How can a boy know what it looks like to behave as a man, love like a man, and be a man in the battle if the main man in his life has abandoned him?

My friend Crawford Loritts works with young men to build their skills as leaders. In his book, *Leadership as an Identity*, he writes that the issue of courage keeps coming up in their conversations:

> Many of [these young men] grapple with fear. . . . I think that the dismantling of our families over the past 50 years or so has almost institutionalized fear and uncertainty. . . . So many of our young men grew up in homes in which they had limited or no contact with their fathers, or they had dads who were detached and didn't provide any meaningful leadership. We are left with a legacy of men who in varying degrees have been feminized. They are uncertain about who and what a man is, and how a man acts and behaves. They are fearful of assuming responsibility and taking the initiative in charting direction. So they take the "road of least resistance" and become passive men.

Storm Number Three: A Culture of Confusion

My son came home one weekend from his university and told me that he had been taught in class that there weren't two sexes but five: male, female, homosexual male, homosexual female, and transgender. No wonder young men are confused and young women are left wondering where the real men are! Male sexuality and identity have become a bewildering array of options.

Think of what it must be like for young boys growing up today. Media outlets and educational elites attack the traditional roles of men and claim that a man who seeks to be a leader in his family is actually oppressing his wife and children. Our culture is permeated with sexuality, where children are exposed to explicit messages and distorted images at a far younger age than their parents were. The educational system doesn't seem to know how to teach boys, and as a result, girls are leaping ahead in test scores, college enrollment (60% are women), and graduation rates.

Boys are increasingly medicated because their parents don't know how to channel their masculinity, adventure and drive.

Is it any wonder that boys grow up so confused? Many have no idea of what it means to be a man and especially a man who cares for a woman in a lifelong marriage relationship.[1]

* While the husband-to-be works through this devotion, the wife-to-be should work through devotion 36. When each of you is done, come together and share what you have learned.

∽ DISCUSS ∽

1. Which of these three storms has most affected you and your ability to step up and be courageous as a man?
2. Read Joshua 1:1-9. What does this passage say is the basis of courageous living?
3. Talk with your fiancée about the kind of men both you and she have had as models growing up. How have those models impacted both you and her? Discuss how they could potentially impact your marriage for good or for bad.
4. Discuss establishing a mentoring relationship with a man who could help you better know how to be the man your future wife needs you to be. Make a short list and pray about establishing a mentee-mentor relationship for one year as you start your marriage.

Note

1. Adapted from *Stepping Up: A Call to Courageous Manhood* by Dennis Rainey (Little Rock, AR: FamilyLife Publishing, 2011). Used by permission.

34

Five *Marks* of a *Man*

(FOR THE HUSBAND-TO-BE)*

*He has told you, O man, what is good; and what does the Lord require of you
but to do justice, and to love kindness, and to walk humbly with your God?*
MICAH 6:8

I'll never forget the young man who came to my front door one Saturday morning. He stood sheepishly and said, "Mr. Rainey, in the past couple of years, I've gotten married and had two children. And I've determined that I don't know how to do marriage. And I don't know how to do family. Could you help me?"

This young man articulated what millions of young men are feeling today—inadequate, fearful and angry and in desperate need of manhood training and vision. They don't know how to do marriage or family.

The Bible paints men as they really are, hiding none of their blemishes or barbaric ways. The honesty of Scripture is one of the reasons I knew that the Bible would be the place to go to learn what a real man should be and do. I began looking through the Scriptures, focusing on passages that talk about men and manhood, and along the way, I discovered five marks of a man:

1. *A man controls his emotions and passions.* Whether single or married, a real man tames his passions. He doesn't abuse women and children; he protects them. He keeps his hands

off a woman who is not his wife, and he treats his wife with love, respect and dignity. He keeps his eyes off pornographic images. He protects a single woman's virginity and innocence. He does not let anger control him. He's a man with a heart, head, conscience and self-control.

2. *A man provides for his family.* First Timothy 5:8 exhorts us, "But if anyone does not provide for his own, and especially for those of his household, he has denied the faith and is worse than an unbeliever" *(NASB)*. These are strident words. When a man doesn't work and provide for his family, he feels a sense of shame. His self-worth sinks. A man who doesn't work, who can't keep a job, who moves from job to job or who refuses to assume his responsibility creates insecurity in his wife and children. Every man needs to provide for his family.

   I find that most men feel a natural sense of responsibility in this area, but many don't seem to understand that providing for their family means more than meeting physical needs. It also means taking responsibility to provide for emotional and spiritual needs. A father should train his children and prepare them to become responsible adults who know how to negotiate the swift and sometimes evil currents of culture.

3. *A man protects his family.* To elaborate on an illustration from John Piper on the essence of masculinity: When you are lying in bed with your wife, and you hear the sound of a window being opened in your kitchen at 3 a.m., do you shake her awake and say, "The last time this occurred, I was the one who took our baseball bat and investigated to see if someone was breaking into our house. Now it's your turn, Sweetheart. Here's the bat!"?

No! That's when the man gets up. One hundred times out of 100 times! Being a protector calls for more than ensuring physical safety. Proverbs 4:10-15 describes a father who protects his son by passing on wisdom, helping him build godly character and teaching him to reject the lies and temptations of the world. This father is protecting not only his son but also the generations to follow as the wisdom he shares gets passed on and on.

4. *A man serves and leads his family.* Those two words—"serves" and "leads"—may seem like a contradiction, but they are inseparable according to Scripture. While the apostle Paul tells us in Ephesians 5:23 that "the husband is the head of the wife," he quickly puts to rest any notions that this leadership allows any form of selfish male dominance. He completes the sentence with "as Christ also is the head of the church." Then the passage goes on to say that husbands should love their wives "just as Christ also loved the church and gave Himself up for her" (verse 25).

This paints a picture of leadership that is contrary to how the world views it. A man is called to be a servant-leader—to take responsibility for his wife and children and to put their needs ahead of his own. He is called to demonstrate selfless, sacrificial love—the type of love God has toward His children.

5. *A man follows God's design for true masculinity.* Micah 6:8 tells us, "He has told you, O man, what is good; and what does the Lord require of you but to do justice, and to love kindness, and to walk humbly with your God?" The core of a man's life should be his relationship with God. The man who walks humbly with God is motivated and

empowered to step up and assume the difficult responsibilities that come his way.

A real man isn't arrogant and doesn't demand his own way. The courageous man is never off duty. [1]

* While the husband-to-be works through this devotion, the wife-to-be should work through devotion 37. When each of you is done, come together and share what you have learned.

∽ DISCUSS ∽

1. How do you feel about the prospect of getting married and becoming a husband? Do you feel prepared? Why? Why not?

2. Read through the five marks of a man. How familiar are these biblical responsibilities to you? Which one is your greatest strength? Weakness?

3. In what areas do you need to step up and be courageous? Practically speaking, what does that look like? Ask your fiancée what she needs in this area from you?

4. Pray that God will give you the strength, wisdom and passion to be His man—a husband who knows his job description and does it.

Note

1. Adapted from *Stepping Up: A Call to Courageous Manhood* by Dennis Rainey (Little Rock, AR: FamilyLife Publishing, 2011). Used by permission.

35

Becoming a
Spiritual Leader

(FOR THE HUSBAND-TO-BE)*

*You shall love the Lord your God with all your heart
and with all your soul and with all your might. And these words
that I command you today shall be on your heart.*
DEUTERONOMY 6:5-6

> "My dad is 75 years old. I haven't talked to him today," [my friend
> said.] "I'll guarantee you my dad got up at 5:30 this morning,
> went downstairs, turned on the coffee maker, went over and
> got his *Thompson Chain Reference Bible,* got his coffee, went up-
> stairs, and spent the first hour this morning in the Word and
> prayer. My dad prayed for me this morning, I'll guarantee you."

My friend was Steve Farrar; and my cohost, Bob Lepine, and I were
interviewing him for our *FamilyLife Today* radio program. We couldn't
resist testing Steve's guarantee, so we called his father, Jim Farrar.

We quickly learned that Steve was wrong! When we asked Jim where
he was at 5:30 that morning, he replied, "I was going out to teach a
Bible study."

So Steve asked his dad where he had been at 5:30 a.m. the day
before. Sure enough, he had been studying his Bible and praying. He
said he'd be doing the same thing the following day.

I asked Jim how long he'd been doing this.

"Oh, man, . . . it's been years and years," he replied.

Steve broke in. "It's been at least 45 years . . . because I remember as a little boy waking up early and seeing him."

Perhaps even more important, Steve established this same routine of beginning each day by reading His Bible and praying. He told us about a Saturday morning when one of his sons, Josh, woke up early and came downstairs to find his father already up.

"Dad, what are you doing?" Josh asked. Steve replied that he was reading the Word. . . . A few minutes later, he said: "Hey, Dad, you ever read the Bible all the way through?" I said, "Yes. . . . "How many times have you done that?" I said, "I don't know—eight, nine, ten times."

He couldn't believe it. . . . [But he was even more astonished when Steve told him], "You'll do that when you're a dad." He said, "I will?" I said, "Oh, yes. . . . That's what Farrar guys do," Steve said.

Many men, as they approach marriage, are apprehensive and unsure about the position of spiritual leadership God has given them in the home. What does it mean? What should they do?

But when I look at men like Jim Farrar, I see the answer: You take the initiative to pursue God. You model a life of purity, godliness and doing what's right. You become a model of a man who serves and loves your wife and children.

You don't need to know the Bible better than your wife. You don't need to be a teacher. You don't need to be eloquent in your prayers. What you do need to do is step up and initiate a relationship with God and engage in the lifetime process of getting to know Him.

Like most men, when I married, I was unsure about what "spiritual leadership" meant. I felt pressure, because I knew Barbara expected me to lead us in studying the Bible, and over the years I've done that, though not as regularly as she had originally hoped.

More important, I've focused on two things as a spiritual leader. Both principles come from Deuteronomy 6:5-9:

> You shall love the Lord your God with all your heart and with all your soul and with all your might. And these words that I command you today shall be on your heart. You shall teach them diligently to your children, and shall talk of them when you sit in your house, and when you walk by the way, and when you lie down, and when you rise. You shall bind them as a sign on your hand, and they shall be as frontlets between your eyes. You shall write them on the doorposts of your house and on your gates.

First, *I've focused on becoming a man of God.* I want my life to reflect verses 5-6 of Deuteronomy 6; I want God and His Word to be the absolute focus of my life. I need to read and study God's Word and seek Him with my whole heart.

Second, *I've focused on being intentional in having my wife and my children join me in pursuing a relationship with God.* In an earlier devotion I wrote about praying daily with Barbara—that has been a vital foundation for our marriage. But Deuteronomy 6:7-9 is also an exhortation to teach God's Word to my family and to talk about it in the natural course of the day—"when you sit in your house, and when you walk by the way." This means talking about God and His Word and applying it to the situations faced in life.

When I read the first few books of Proverbs, I am impressed by the words of a father who called his son to "be attentive to my wisdom . . . that you may keep discretion, and your lips may guard knowledge" (Proverbs 5:1-2). This father applied God's Word to very practical situations such as handling money and avoiding the "forbidden woman"

(Proverbs 2:16; 5:3,20; 7:5). Over the years of raising my children, I initiated many conversations on topics like this to pass on biblical wisdom.

Being a spiritual leader in your family may involve some regular times of Bible study, worship and prayer. In fact, I'm hoping that you enjoy this devotional so much that you make this type of experience a regular part of your marriage. (Check out our devotional *Moments Together for Couples*. We think you will really like using it as you begin your marriage.) But I think those times will flow out of something more critical—your walk with God and your determination to help your wife and family seek Him as you do.

* While the husband-to-be works through this devotion, the wife-to-be should work through devotion 38. When each of you is done, come together and share what you have learned.

∽ DISCUSS ∽

1. Ask your wife-to-be what her expectations are of you being the spiritual leader of her and your family. Tell her not to be embarrassed if she doesn't have any concrete things to share—you just want to know what she's looking for from you as a spiritual leader.

2. When you have thought in the past of a husband's role as a spiritual leader, how have you envisioned this responsibility? How do you envision it now?

3. Pray together, asking God to give you the ongoing conviction to make Him and His Word the focus of your lives.

36

Essential Number One:
Make *God's Word* a Priority

(FOR THE WIFE-TO-BE)
BY BARBARA RAINEY

Give me understanding, that I may keep your law
and observe it with my whole heart.
PSALM 119:34

I'm now in a season of life where I have more time to think. I've been through the honeymoon years of marriage and the years of raising six children. The child-rearing years were so busy that I was swamped in dailiness of life and I couldn't ever pull back long enough to look at the big picture.

Recently, though, I've been thinking about the absolute necessities for a married woman; and time has helped me realize there are just a few essentials. Like a pot of soup left simmering in order to reduce the liquid, my years have condensed the necessary ingredients for married women to just a few. As you begin your marriage, you have the opportunity to make these essentials the foundation of your married life and relationship.

The first essential is to *be in God's Word*. Make God's Word a priority in your life now—before your life becomes more complicated. The Word of God is so rich, so filled with wisdom and power, that you should consider it as important to life as food and water.

For me, regular time in God's Word was a huge challenge when I was raising my children. Though my goal was to read the Bible regularly, I felt very frustrated and defeated much of the time. For one thing, my kids would often interrupt my reading. And when I'd try to get up early to read the Bible, I'd find that one of my children had gotten up earlier and needed my attention. Or I'd be so tired that I couldn't focus on the words I was trying to read.

Once my children were older and finally all in school, I was able to control my time a little more. We were pushing 20 years of marriage, and I understood as never before how important it was for me to be in God's Word for myself, instead of depending on second-hand information from sermons, from books I was reading or even from friends who talked about what they were learning. As I finally began to consistently read and study the Bible, I realized that God could speak to me . . . He *wanted* to speak to me!

As a result, I promised myself that I would be in regular, serious, inductive Bible study until I breathe my last breath. I have learned that if I don't have the accountability of a class and an assignment that has to be done on a weekly basis, it's too easy for me to put it off.

And here's what may be a new thought for you: I believe God wants us women to be theologians. Have you ever thought of yourself as a theologian? Probably not. But theology is simply the study of God—knowing who He is. When we study God's Word, we get to know Him personally and develop a relationship with Him. Therefore, we understand better why He does what He does.

One fall I attended a women's conference where I heard John Piper, pastor of Bethlehem Baptist Church in Minneapolis, say this: "Wimpy theology makes wimpy women." I want to be a strong woman. I want my strength to come from a one-on-one relationship with God.

I discovered why strong theology is so important in June 2008 when our granddaughter, Molly, died after seven days of life. During that week in the hospital with my daughter and son-in-law, I found myself reading the Bible constantly to find what was true in a terribly difficult circumstance.

Over and over I read Psalm 139:15-16: "My frame was not hidden from You, when I was made in secret, and skillfully wrought in the depths of the earth; Your eyes have seen my unformed substance *(NASB)*." God was in control. This was not a mistake. He knit Molly's body together in my daughter's womb; He made her the way He wanted to make her.

Psalm 139 goes on to say, "In Your book were all written the days that were ordained for me, when as yet there was not one of them" (verse 16, *NASB*). Even though that week was a very painful time in our lives, we were confident that God had formed Molly, knew the number of her days and had purposed her life, even though it was short.

God's Word was our anchor during that week. God's Word became our strength.

God's Word is the only thing that will make you strong in the storms of life.

∽ DISCUSS ∽

1. Read Psalm 119. You will find it full of benefits—God's promises that come from making time to read God's Word. Write down some of the benefits you find in just one passage: verses 105-112.

2. How would you benefit from spending more time in God's Word than you do now?

3. What is keeping you from regularly spending time in God's Word?

4. Share with your husband-to-be what you've learned from this devotion.

5. Pray together that God's Word would become the anchor of your relationship.

37

Essential Number Two:
Love *Your Husband* Unconditionally

(FOR THE WIFE-TO-BE)
BY BARBARA RAINEY

Love bears all things, believes all things, hopes all things, endures all things.
1 CORINTHIANS 13:7

I remember when I first realized that Dennis was not like my father.

My dad was an all-American "Mr. Fixit." He was vice president in charge of maintenance at a large steel plant, and at home he could do anything. He loved working around the house and the yard—making repairs, painting, tinkering on the car.

Dennis, on the other hand, declared, "If you can't fix something with baling wire and duct tape, you should throw it away and get a new one." He disliked working around the house, preferring to spend his spare time watching sports on television.

I remember those early days in our marriage. Dennis would plop into his easy chair in front of the TV, and I would circle him like a vulture, trying to give him a gentle hint of how I felt he could better use his time.

Dennis and I have come a long way since then. He's still not Mr. Fixit, but he tries. And somewhere along the way he developed an enjoyment of gardening, so he could spend time with me.

Meanwhile, I've learned an important lesson: *It's important to love my husband unconditionally.* This is a second essential for every Christian wife. I need to receive Dennis as a gift from God—no matter how different he is from me or from what I expected.

I had an opportunity to apply this lesson in our first month of marriage. So get ready. Practicing this happens quickly and often! Dennis took the initiative to make a small financial investment, and we ended up losing money. As we talked it over and I shared my disappointment, it was obvious that Dennis knew he had made a poor choice.

In that moment I faced a choice of my own: Would I accept Dennis as my husband, or would I nag him and make him feel like a failure? Even as a young Christian I knew enough to know that God wanted to use this for good for my husband. I needed to get out of God's way and let Him work in my husband's life.

At times like this, a wife learns that love is not all feelings. This is when you honor your wedding vows and say, "I'm committed to you, no matter what."

Another challenge for Dennis and me when we married was how different we are. The old adage that opposites attract is really true for us. For instance, Dennis is impulsive. He gets an idea and he'll be gone. I, on the other hand, tend to be very disciplined; I like to think and evaluate before I act. During our first year of marriage, I often found myself left in Dennis's dust.

I remember praying diligently for God to change all the things in Dennis I didn't like. Then I realized what really needed to be changed was my attitude. I needed to ask God to make me content not only with Dennis as he was, but also with the positive sides of our differences. God did change my perspective, and in time I began to see how much I need my husband's spontaneity to balance my more rigid control.

Another difference that soon became apparent in our marriage was that my husband had a stronger sexual drive than me. I turned a corner in our relationship when I chose to begin thanking God for how He designed both of us. I realized how important it was for Dennis to need me, and how our coming together physically gives both of us the comfort of being known and accepted on a level deeper than that of any other human relationship. So I began making it a greater priority to express my unconditional love for Dennis sexually.

I choose to love my husband, even if I don't have strong feelings. Ultimately, love is a commitment to seek the best of the one loved. I can choose to exercise my power as a passionate, nurturing, fully alive woman; or I can withhold and withdraw.

Do you realize that your husband-to-be will never be the man God created him to be without your full and unconditional acceptance? You are God's primary instrument of love and affirmation. You have the power to make your future husband or break him, because *men are not born, they are made.*

✎ DISCUSS ✎

1. Read Romans 5:8 and John 15:12. What do you think it means to love your future spouse as God loves you?

2. Read 1 Corinthians 13:4-8. Choose three descriptions of love from this passage and answer the following question by filling in the blank with one of the descriptions: How can I show _____ as I seek to love my future husband unconditionally?

3. What are some differences between you and your husband-to-be that you predict may be difficult for you to accept unconditionally after you're married? Discuss with your fiancé what he needs from you in those situations.

4. Pray that God will give you the ability to trust Him for your differences and to find creative ways to show unconditional love in your marriage.

38

Essential Number Three:
Become a Helper
to Your Husband

(FOR THE WIFE-TO-BE)
BY BARBARA RAINEY

For man was not made from woman, but woman from man. Neither was man created for woman, but woman for man.
1 CORINTHIANS 11:8-9

For years, Dennis and I talked about moving to a rural area just outside Little Rock. Our children were young at the time, and the thought of giving them room to roam was inviting. But it felt like a risk. What if we didn't like driving back and forth to town? What if we felt isolated from our friends and our church?

We were stuck in a logjam, unable to make a decision. And in the process I sensed that Dennis felt a bit paralyzed, because he was afraid of making a wrong decision. There's a lot of pressure on a man as he attempts to lead his family, and it's easy for a husband to avoid risk because of a fear of failure.

Finally one day I asked Dennis, "So what if we decide we don't like living in the country? We can sell and move back to town!"

Somehow my words freed the logjam. Dennis realized that even a wrong decision really wouldn't matter. We decided to make the move, and we loved it immediately.

Looking back, I think I helped Dennis on a couple of levels. First, I provided perspective. This was not a life-and-death issue, and it wasn't worth so much angst and introspection. Second, I gave Dennis the freedom to fail; and in doing so, I affirmed him in his role as a husband and father.

While all of us are called to be helpers to others, the Bible places a special emphasis on this responsibility for wives. First Corinthians 11:8-9 points out that a woman was created "for man." Paul's words affirm the creation of woman described in Genesis 2:18: The woman was a "helper fit for him." *Being a helper* is a third essential for Christian wives.

It is interesting to note that this is also part of the job description of the Holy Spirit, who is often referred to as Helper. For example, Jesus told the disciples that, after He died, His heavenly Father would send the Holy Spirit after His death: "And I will ask the Father and he will give you another Helper, to be with you forever, even the Spirit of truth" (John 14:16-17).

The fact that "helper" is applied to a wife signifies that we women have been given tremendous power for good in our husbands' lives. God has designed wives to help their husbands become all that God intends for them to be.

Here's an interesting exercise: Read through passages about the Holy Spirit in the New Testament and ask yourself, "How can I help my husband in a similar way?" You can never be the Holy Spirit in your husband's life, of course, but it is possible to find inspiration in the descriptions of what the Holy Spirit does in our lives.

For example, Jesus said that the Spirit would "bring to your remembrance all that I have said to you" (John 14:26). He was speaking of how the Spirit would, in a supernatural way, help the disciples remember His words after His death and resurrection. In a similar way, I think that as a wife you can bring to your husband's remembrance the truth of Christ and the truth of God's Word in his life.

Romans 8:26 tells us that "the Spirit helps us in our weakness. For we do not know what to pray for as we ought, but the Spirit himself intercedes for us." I think one of the great callings of wives is to intercede and pray for our husbands. Praying for our husbands—for all they are facing and all that God has called them to do—is one of the greatest gifts we can give them in our role as helper.

There are many more ways for wives to help husbands. For example:

- *Meet his "aloneness" need.* Remember that God said it was not good for man to be alone. God intentionally created the first man with an aloneness need, and your husband is just as incomplete. God brought you into his life to meet his need for companionship and to call him away from being an independent spirit.
- *Build him up.* Most men are more insecure than they let on. They need continual affirmation and encouragement as they strive to follow God and His call for their lives.
- *Take pressure off him and give him a respite of peace and love in a hostile world.* As author Tricia Goyer says, "A good meal and a warm wife can wash away every other care in the world."
- *Find ways to please him.* Become a student of your husband and become an expert on what encourages him, what makes him happy, what energizes him.

Remember, it takes years for a man to become a strong husband. Be patient with him. Put aside your high expectations of how a perfect husband would lead his family spiritually, behave socially or perform intellectually. Keep your hope in God, not in your man. Then you will not be disappointed.

∽ Discuss ∽

1. What are some ways that you can see clearly today that your husband-to-be needs you?

2. Make a list of how you've seen God use you to help your future husband in some of these areas:

   - Helping him gain perspective
   - Reminding him of God's Word
   - Encouraging him to take risks
   - Pleasing him
   - Building him up and encouraging him
   - Meeting his "aloneness" need

3. In what ways will you, as a wife, be able to help your husband like nobody else can?

4. Pray that God would give you powerful and creative ideas for helping your husband after you are married.

39

Who Does the *Housework?*

*Clothe yourselves, all of you, with humility toward one another, for
"God opposes the proud but gives grace to the humble."*
1 PETER 5:5

"I would love to find out how to get my husband to do some
work around the house. The problem we have is that he wants
to mess up, and then fuss about the house not being together
[clean]."

"For my husband and I, we have decided that whomever is
home more gets more housework."

"My husband and I picked our chores based on what we were
good at and what we liked to do."

If you think about it, some of the most common practical decisions
you will make early in your marriage revolve around who does what.
When you live in a home together, there are a multitude of chores to
complete. Who cuts the grass? Who buys the food and cooks? Who vac-
uums? Who cleans the toilets? Who pays the bills? Who feeds the dog?

And this is all *before* you have children.

Dividing up housework is a big issue in marriages today. A 2007
survey by the Pew Research Center indicated that 62 percent of Americans
ranked "sharing household chores" as "very important for a successful

marriage."[1] Sharing housework ranked higher than factors such as adequate income, shared religious beliefs, and children. In fact, when FamilyLife ran an article about this topic on our website and asked for reader responses, we received 85 long emails in just a few hours.

For many years surveys have shown that wives typically do much more of the housework than husbands, even when both spouses are employed full-time. This has been changing with each generation, however, and many couples today report that husbands share the burden.

But how do you divide that burden equally? Is that even possible?

We often hear in our culture that marriage should be a 50/50 relationship, where each spouse strives to do his or her share. The 50/50 Plan in marriage says, "You do your part, and I'll do mine." But when you try to apply that standard to a practical area like household chores, you quickly realize that 50/50 just doesn't work. As one wife wrote in an email, "There is no way to split anything down the middle as far as housework goes."

The biggest weakness of the 50/50 Plan is simple: *It is impossible to determine if your spouse has met you halfway . . . and the person who says he'll meet you half way is usually a poor judge of distance!* Because it is unlikely that you can agree on where halfway is, each is left to scrutinize the other's performance from a jaded and often selfish perspective.

Instead, marriage works when you both have a 100/100 philosophy, which requires a 100 percent effort from each of you. Start by stating the 100/100 Plan like this: "I will do what I can to love you without demanding an equal amount in return." Yes, there will be times when one person appears to get the advantage in the relationship. And there will be times when, because of sickness or injury or unusual circumstances, one of you will need to shoulder 99 percent of the load. But love requires sacrifice. Stick with the 100/100 Plan, and you will see increasing cooperation and intimacy in your marriage.

One of our readers told us:

God has blessed me with a very loving husband who does not see that there is a division for the daily upkeep of *our* home. I am a stay-at-home mom now, but my husband has always helped with domestic duties . . . We are on the same team; there is no place for "your job" or "my job." It's "our job." I cannot end this without saying that my husband has truly mastered the art of loving and serving as the Bible says in Ephesians 5. He daily looks for ways to ease my stress and help my day be brighter."

One theme that came through loud and clear in many of the emails we received is that a marriage thrives when both husband and wife seek to love and serve each other. One husband wrote, "I see helping in the housework is one of the easiest and most tangible ways to serve my wife. Anything to lessen her burden."

Another added, "As the man, my primary responsibility is love. I have found that my wife receives a great deal of love when I contribute to chores. As the man, I bite the bullet, and do the chores I don't like to do for my wife in love. This has been a very successful way for me to shower love on my wife."

❧ DISCUSS ❧

1. How was household work divided among family members as you were growing up?

2. Take a few minutes now to talk about who will do what in your home after you are married. Make a list of chores that will be required. Talk about which chores you feel you are good at doing, which chores you enjoy and which chores you hate. Talk about the standards you want to establish for your home—organization, cleanliness, etc. —and be realistic about your expectations.

3. Read 1 Peter 5:5-7. In this spirit, how can you follow the 100/100 Plan as you divide household chores?

4. In what other areas of your marriage will you need to follow the 100/100 Plan?

5. Pray together that God will give both of you the attitude of a servant and the humility you need to follow the 100/100 Plan.

Note

1. Paul Taylor, Cary Funk and April Clark. *As Marriage and Parenthood Drift Apart, Public Is Concerned About Social Impact* (Washington, DC: Pew Research Center, 2007), p. 2. http://www.pewsocialtrends.org/files/2007/07/ Pew-Marriage-report-6-28-for-web-display.pdf

40

Making *Decisions* as a *Couple*

How good and pleasant it is when God's people live together in unity!
PSALM 133:1 (*NIV*)

Whenever we talk about teamwork in marriage, one of the most common questions we hear is, "How do you make decisions, especially when you differ and disagree?"

This is one of those gritty issues in marriage. Differing values, priorities, personalities, spiritual maturity, family backgrounds, understanding of biblical roles and responsibilities—they all come together in the multitude of decisions you will make together as a couple. And this is one of the great tests of oneness in marriage.

Especially when you disagree.

When someone asks Barbara and me what we do when we disagree on a decision, our answer is: We believe it is clear that the Bible teaches that the husband is ultimately responsible for the direction of the marriage and family. Ephesians 5:22-23 clearly spells this out: "Wives, submit to your own husbands, as to the Lord. For the husband is the head of the wife even as Christ is the head of the church, his body, and is himself its Savior." As the "head" of his wife, the husband has the responsibility to listen carefully to his wife and her perspective, go prayerfully with his wife before God and consider the circumstances,

DENNIS & BARBARA RAINEY

and lead them in making a decision. If they can't come to an agreement, it falls upon him to make a decision.

Sounds pretty clear, doesn't it? But there's an additional perspective we need to add: There have only been a handful of times in over 41 years of marriage when we haven't been able to reach a consensus and I have made the final decision. And that's the real love story here.

If you are operating in harmony as a couple, you will not face many decisions on which you strongly disagree. We've disagreed with one another hundreds of times, but we've taken the time to understand where the other person is coming from, and we've usually worked the issue out.

The following are a few principles that we've practiced over the years that have helped us make decisions:

1. *At all times, seek to check your selfishness and pride.* It's interesting to note how often the concept of unity and harmony in the Scriptures is tied to humility. First Peter 3:8, for example, tells us, "Finally, all of you, have unity of mind, sympathy, brotherly love, a tender heart, and a humble mind." It's important for both of you to truly be humble and "hear" your spouse's perspective—and to consider what God's will truly is in the situation.

2. *Decide together on your core family values.* By "values," I mean what is important to you. How will you measure success in your marriage and family? What values are you truly living for? What set of core convictions will determine how big a house you will live in or what kind of car to drive? What values will drive decisions on how much money to give away or how many extra hours you will work each week if that means more time away from your children?

When we began to list our values early in marriage, we suddenly realized we were distilling the essence of our lives—who we were, our convictions and what we were about. Here is the order of our big-picture values:

- Our personal relationship with God
- Our marriage
- Our children

All other issues, such as decisions relating to vocation and career, are evaluated in light of their impact on these three supreme priorities. We agreed that no other success would matter if we failed on these three.

Once we decided the big issues, we each wrote down the top five values that were important to us as individuals, and then we compared our lists. We discovered that a number of our values were different, which revealed why we were feeling some pressure and tension in our marriage.

For example, one of my top values was building relationships, but that wasn't even in Barbara's top five! She had listed "work ethic" as one of her most important values, but that wasn't on my top five list. We then sat down and hammered out what became our "Top Five Values" list. This exercise gave us the opportunity to understand each other better, and all these values helped us through the years as we've made various decisions.

3. *Generally defer to each other in your areas of responsibility.* In many situations with the children, for example, Barbara will be far more versed and have much more insight into what is going on with each child emotionally and circumstantially. I may disagree with her on something,

but usually I try to defer to her intuition in whatever the situation is. In a similar way, Barbara has not been as close to the finances as I've been, and in this area she has frequently deferred to me and my wisdom.

4. *If you can't come to a consensus, trust in God to give the husband the wisdom to make the right choice.* You will be surprised how often you will come to a consensus on your decisions when you work through this process. Nevertheless, on some occasions you will face a stalemate. If you have a roleless marriage—where there is no final authority—the stalemate will produce ambiguity and tension. In such a marriage, the stronger personality usually wins the power struggle.

We feel more comfortable trusting in God to work through the husband in these situations. This doesn't mean that the husband has permission to choose his own way—he is still bound by his responsibilities to treat his wife as a fellow heir in Christ and love her as Christ loves the Church.

☙ DISCUSS ❧

Answer the following questions individually, and then discuss them as a couple:

1. Read Ephesians 4:2-3; Philippians 2:1-3; and 1 Peter 3:8. How would you apply these passages to the task of making decisions together as a couple?

2. What's an example of a time when you disagreed on a decision and came to a consensus that pleased both of you?

3. If you can, list one or two occasions when you operated from wrong motives and forced a decision on your future spouse.

4. Are there any issues facing you now where you are stuck in a disagreement? How could the principles from this devotion help you in this decision?

5. After sharing your answers with each other, pray that God will give you humility and unity in the decisions you make together in the time before your marriage—and afterwards.

41

Keep on *Running*

Let us run with endurance the race that is set before us.
HEBREWS 12:1

Here's the irony: To many couples, engagement feels like a full-out sprint to the finish line of the wedding day. And yet marriage is just the beginning and it's *not* a sprint—it's a long-distance race.

For years I've been running for exercise, and one thing I've learned is you can't run long distance unless you train for it. You need to stay in shape.

Hebrews 12:1-3 describes life itself as a race when it tells us to "run with endurance the race that is set before us" (verse 1). And it offers some practical advice on long-distance running that, if followed, will have a huge impact on your marriage.

First, *"lay aside every weight, and sin which clings so closely"* (verse 1). Try running sometime while carrying a five-pound weight in each hand. You won't make it far. Living with sin has the same impact on the race of life. Make a commitment to live a life of continual repentance—applying the words of 1 John 1:9 to your life every day: "If we confess our sins, he is faithful and just to forgive us our sins and to cleanse us from all unrighteousness."

Second, *cultivate your relationship with Jesus.* Hebrews 12:2 urges you to run the race with our eyes "looking to Jesus, the founder and perfecter of our faith." He is the One who endured the cross so that you could be redeemed. And He longs for a close relationship with you. He is the

DENNIS & BARBARA RAINEY

bread of life, and through Him you gain the sustenance you need—as an individual and as a couple—to run with endurance.

Our hope is that this devotional has given you a glimpse of a spiritual bond with your future spouse that is possible through your relationship with God. As you begin your marriage, continue spending time together reading God's Word and praying. In fact, one good way to continue this devotional experience is by reading our two devotionals for couples: *Moments Together for Couples* and *Moments with You*.

Continuing my running metaphor, I'd like to offer a few other suggestions on lifelong endurance in marriage:

1. *Don't run alone.* I've noticed that when I run with others, the effort feels easier. I suppose it's a mix of adrenaline and the simple fact that the presence of other runners encourages me to focus on something different from my fatigue. In the same way, you need the encouragement of other couples who are committed to walking with God and to fulfilling their marriage vows. One way of doing this is to be a part of a small group of couples that you'd like to do life with. Consider forming such a group at your church, if one doesn't already exist. (Also check out The Art of Marriage® Small Group video series and The Home-Builders Couples Series (small groups) at familylife.com.)

2. *Find a coach.* FamilyLife once commissioned some focus groups to learn what young couples wanted to help them make their marriages and families successful. The answer? They wanted a person (or a couple), someone with skin on: a mentor. They were facing issues they didn't expect—issues they knew they couldn't handle without some help—and they longed for an older couple who could guide them through the formative years of their marriage

and raising a family. One of the most important things you can do to start your marriage right is to establish a mentoring relationship with another couple for the first 12 to 24 months.

Certainly you need access to your pastor, but even more important you need to connect with an older couple. After your wedding an older couple can help you when you reach any rough patches—when you are tempted to be bitter or resentful. They can help you with *perspective*— about how to weather the storms and how to keep romance and sex alive.

3. *Don't stop learning.* Just as a good runner will keep up with the latest information about nutrition, training and technique, you as a couple need to look for ways to keep your relationship fresh and strong. Consider going in for a "12-month checkup"—perhaps at one of FamilyLife's Weekend to Remember getaways (go to weekendtoremember.com for more information). It's a great way to keep fit.

4. *Remember others are watching you run.* Ultimately you should look out to the world and ask, "What can we be doing together to advance God's kingdom?" Part of running God's race means embracing His mission for you as a couple. And part of that mission is the influence your marriage can have in a culture of people who are desperate to see a real relationship that goes the distance. When you commit your life to your God and to your spouse, there are people watching—parents, grandparents, friends, coworkers, neighbors and your children (if and when you have them). Your marriage will have a profound impact on all of them.

No matter what obstacles you face during your long-distance run, don't stop running and don't stop training. As much as you enjoy each other now, remember that the joy of persevering and finishing the race together is even greater.

∾ DISCUSS ∾

1. Read Hebrews 12:1-3; 1 Peter 1:22; and Ephesians 2:10. What do these passages tell you about the secrets of persevering in marriage?

2. Discuss what your mission is as a couple. How would you like to see God use you two to impact others for His purposes?

3. Ask God to lead, bless, provide and sustain your commitment and love for each other. And ask God to use you as a couple to impact others.

Appendix

The *Secret* to *Building* a Great *Marriage* and *Family*

Your life is basically normal—at least most of the time. You are moving closer to marriage, and you think you couldn't be happier.

You've been learning about building a marriage upon a foundation of God's Word. The relationship with your future spouse is going well. (Okay, maybe it isn't perfect, but what relationship is?) But for some reason, there's a nagging feeling deep inside you, hinting that there's something more. That you're still lacking something. That you're missing the basic issue at the heart of every problem in every marriage. That there's a secret to building the type of marriage and family relationships you desire.

Do you want to know the secret to building the type of marriage and family relationships you desire?

The secret is this: *If you want to experience marriage the way it was designed to be, you need a vital relationship with the God who created you and offers you the power to live a life of joy and purpose.*

Jesus Christ said, "I came that they might have life, and have it abundantly" (John 10:10). And Psalm 16:11 tells us, "In [God's] presence is "fullness of joy." God gives us a biblical plan for making family relationships work, and He gives us the power to follow that plan through a relationship with Him.

DENNIS & BARBARA RAINEY

Recognizing the Problem

There is a problem we all face, however. It's a problem that prevents us from establishing a relationship with a holy God, no matter how hard we try. That problem is sin.

In our world today, "sin" is not a popular word. Many people have little idea what sin is. Put simply, sin is a term that means missing the target, or missing the mark. Romans 3:23 tells us, "For all have sinned and fall short of the glory of God."

Most of us have assumed throughout our lives that the term "sin" refers only to the really bad acts, like murder. But in reality, sin is anything that breaks God's laws, and it is impossible to go through life without sinning. Look at the 10 Commandments, for example. Here are three of them from Exodus 20:3-17:

- You shall not take the name of the Lord your God in vain.
- You shall not steal.
- You shall not bear false witness against your neighbor.

If you have broken any of these commandments—even told little "white lies" or stolen something small, like envelopes from work or a pen that doesn't belong to you—then you are guilty of breaking God's laws. And it is that sin that creates a gap between you and God.

None of us has trusted and treasured God the way we should. We have sought to satisfy ourselves with other things and have treated those things as more valuable than God. We have gone our own way.

According to the Bible, we have to pay a penalty for our sins. We cannot simply do things the way we choose and hope it will all be okay with God. Following our own plans leads to our destruction. Proverbs 14:12 tells us, "There is a way that seems right to a man, but its end is the way to death." And Romans 6:23 says, "The wages of sin is death."

The penalty for sin is eternal punishment and separation from God. And no matter how hard we try, we cannot make up for the sins that we have committed. God is holy, and we are sinful. In order to enter heaven, God demands perfection, and we have already seen that no one can be perfect. No matter how hard we try, we cannot come up with some plan, like living a good life or even trying to do what the Bible says, to avoid the penalty for having sinned.

Paying the Penalty

Thankfully, God has a way to solve our dilemma. He became a man through the person of Jesus Christ. He lived a holy and perfect life in obedience to God's plan. He also willingly died on a cross to pay our penalty for having sinned. Then He proved that He is more powerful than sin or death by rising from the dead. He alone has the power to overrule the penalty for our sins.

> Jesus said to him, "I am the way, and the truth, and the life. No one comes to the Father except through me" (John 14:6).

> But God shows his love for us in that while we were still sinners, Christ died for us (Romans 5:8).

> The wages of sin is death, but the free gift of God is eternal life in Christ Jesus our Lord (Romans 6:23).

> Christ died for our sins, . . . he was buried, . . . he was raised on the third day in accordance with the Scriptures, and that he appeared to Cephas, then to the twelve. Then he appeared to more than five hundred (1 Corinthians 15:3-6).

The death and resurrection of Jesus has fixed our sin problem. He bridged the gap between God and us. He calls all of us to come to

Him and to give up our own flawed plans for how to run our lives. He wants us to trust God and His plan.

Accepting God's Solution

If you agree that you are separated from God, He calls you to confess your sins. All of us have made messes of our lives, because we have stubbornly preferred our ideas and plans over God's. As a result, we deserve to be cut off from God's love and His care for us. But God has promised that if we will agree that we have rebelled against His plan for us and have messed up our lives, He will forgive us and will fix our sin problem:

> To all who did receive him, who believed in his name, he gave the right to become children of God (John 1:12).

> For by grace you have been saved through faith. And this is not your own doing; it is the gift of God, not a result of works, so that no one may boast (Ephesians 2:8-9).

When we "receive" Christ, we acknowledge that we are sinners and that we can't fix the problem ourselves. It means we turn away from our sins. And it means we trust Christ to forgive our sins and to make us the kind of people He wants us to be. It's not enough to just intellectually believe that Christ is the Son of God. We must by faith—as an act of the will—trust in Him and His plans for our lives.

Are things right between you and God? Are God and His plan at the center of your life? Or is life spinning out of control as you seek to make your way on your own?

You can decide today to make a change. You can turn to Christ and allow Him to transform your life. All you need to do is to talk to Him and tell Him what is stirring in your mind and in your heart. If you've never done this before, consider taking these steps:

1. Do you agree that you need God? Admit your need to God.

2. Have you made a mess of your life by following your own plan? Acknowledge your situation to God.

3. Do you want God to forgive you? Ask God to forgive you.

4. Do you believe that Jesus' death on the cross and His resurrection from the dead gave Him the power to fix your sin problem and to grant you the gift of eternal life? Declare to God your faith in Christ's finished work on the cross and His forgiveness.

5. Are you ready to acknowledge that God's plan for your life is better than any plan you could come up with? Agree with God and His plan.

6. Do you agree that God has the right to be the Lord and master of your life? Surrender, yield and declare to God that you want Jesus Christ to be *your* Master.

Once you've spoken to God, read the following prayer and decide whether it expresses the desire of your heart:

Lord Jesus, I need You. Thank You for dying on the cross for my sins. I receive You as my Savior and Lord. Thank You for forgiving my sins and giving me eternal life. Make me the kind of person You want me to be. Amen.

If this prayer expresses the desire of your heart, pray it right now, and Almighty God will forgive you of your sin and make you His own, just as He promised.

Living the Christian Life

For a person who is a follower of Christ—a Christian—the penalty for sin is paid in full. But the effect of sin continues throughout our lives:

> I do not do the good I want, but the evil I do not want is what I keep on doing (Romans 7:19).

> If we say that we have no sin, we deceive ourselves, and the truth is not in us (1 John 1:8).

The effects of sin carry over into our marriages as well. Even Christians struggle to maintain solid, God-honoring marriages. Most couples eventually realize that they can't do it on their own. But with God's help, they can succeed. The Holy Spirit can have a huge impact in the marriages of Christians who live constantly, moment by moment, under His gracious direction.

Self-Centered Christians

Many Christians struggle to live the Christian life in their own strength, not allowing God to control their lives. Their interests are self-directed, often resulting in failure and frustration.

> But I, brothers, could not address you as spiritual people, but as people of the flesh, as infants in Christ. I fed you with milk, not solid food, for you were not ready for it. And even now you are not yet ready, for you are still of the flesh. For while there is jealousy and strife among you, are you not of the flesh and behaving only in a human way? (1 Corinthians 3:1-3).

Self-centered Christians cannot experience abundant and fruitful Christian lives, because they trust in only their own efforts to live right: They are either uninformed about—or have forgotten—God's love, forgiveness and power. These Christians

- have an up-and-down spiritual experience;
- cannot understand themselves—they want to do what is right but cannot; and
- fail to draw upon the power of the Holy Spirit to follow Christ in their lives.

Some or all of the following traits may characterize Christians who do not fully trust God:

- disobedient
- no love for God and others
- inconsistent prayer life
- no desire for Bible study
- legalistic attitude
- plagued by impure thoughts
- jealous
- worrisome
- easily discouraged or frustrated
- critical
- lack of purpose

In fact, individuals who profess to be Christians but who continue to sin should realize that they may not be Christians at all:

> For you may be sure of this, that everyone who is sexually immoral or impure, or who is covetous (that is, an idolater), has no inheritance in the kingdom of Christ and God (Ephesians 5:5).

By this we know that we have come to know him, if we keep his commandments (1 John 2:3).

No one who abides in him keeps on sinning; no one who keeps on sinning has either seen him or known him. . . . No one born of God makes a practice of sinning, for God's seed abides in him, and he cannot keep on sinning because he has been born of God (1 John 3:6,9).

Spirit-Centered Christians

When Christians put Christ on the throne of their lives, they yield to God's control. The interests of these Christians are directed by the Holy Spirit, resulting in harmony with God's plan.

[Jesus said,] "I am the vine; you are the branches. Whoever abides in me and I in him, he it is that bears much fruit, for apart from me you can do nothing" (John 15:5).

But you will receive power when the Holy Spirit comes upon you; and you will be my witnesses in Jerusalem and in all Judea and Samaria, and to the end of the earth (Acts 1:8).

The fruit of the Spirit is love, joy, peace, patience, kindness, goodness, faithfulness, gentleness, self-control; against such things there is no law (Galatians 5:22-23).

The following traits result naturally from the Holy Spirit's work in the lives of Spirit-centered Christians:

- Christ centered
- Holy Spirit empowered
- motivated to tell others about Jesus

- dedicated to prayer
- studies God's Word
- trusts God
- obeys God
- loving
- joyful
- peaceful
- patient
- kind
- faithful
- gentle
- self-controlled

The degree to which these traits appear in the lives and marriages of Spirit-centered Christians depends upon two things: (1) the extent to which the Christians trust the Lord with every detail of life, and (2) how mature those Christians are in Christ. Of course individuals who are only beginning to understand the ministry of the Holy Spirit should not be discouraged if they are not as fruitful as mature Christians who have known and experienced this truth for a longer period of time.

Giving God Control

Jesus promises His followers abundant and fruitful lives as they allow themselves to be directed and empowered by the Holy Spirit. As you give God control of your life, Christ lives in and through you in the power of the Holy Spirit (see John 15:1-11; Galatians 5:16; Romans 8:11).

If you sincerely desire to be directed and empowered by God, you can turn your life over to the control of the Holy Spirit right now (see Matthew 5:6; John 7:37-39).

First, confess your sins to God, agreeing with Him that you want to turn from any past sinful patterns in your life. Thank God in faith that He has forgiven all of your sins because Christ died for you (see Colossians 2:13-15; 1 John 1:9; 2:1-3; Hebrews 10:1-18).

Next be sure to offer every area of your life to God:

> Therefore I urge you, brethren, by the mercies of God, to present your bodies a living and holy sacrifice, acceptable to God, which is your spiritual service of worship. And do not be conformed to this world, but be transformed by the renewing of your mind, so that you may prove what the will of God is, that which is good and acceptable and perfect (Romans 12:1-2, *NASB*).

Consider what areas you might rather keep to yourself, and be sure you're willing to give God control in those areas.

Then, by faith, commit to live according to the Holy Spirit's guidance and power:

> I say, walk by the Spirit, and you will not gratify the desires of the flesh. For the desires of the flesh are against the Spirit, and the desires of the Spirit are against the flesh, for these are opposed to each other, to keep you from doing the things you want to do (Galatians 5:16-17).

And trust in God's promise:

> This is the confidence that we have toward him, that if we ask anything according to his will he hears us. And if we know that he hears us in whatever we ask, we know that we have the requests that we have asked of him (1 John 5:14-15).

Walking in the Spirit

If you become aware of an area of your life (an attitude or an action) that is displeasing to God, simply confess your sin, and thank God that He has forgiven your sins on the basis of Christ's death on the cross. Accept God's love and forgiveness by faith, and continue to have fellowship with Him and to walk in the Spirit.

Consider practicing this exercise—Spiritual Breathing—as you give control back to God:

- *Exhale.* Confess your sin. Agree with God that you've sinned against Him, and thank Him for His forgiveness of it. Remember that confession involves repentance, a determination to change attitudes and actions.
- *Inhale.* Surrender control of your life to Christ, inviting the Holy Spirit to once again take charge. Trust that He now directs and empowers you. Returning to your faith in God enables you to continue to experience God's love and forgiveness.

This is the essence of walking in the Spirit—exhaling and inhaling, maintaining an attitude of repentance hour by hour, day by day.

Revolutionizing Your Marriage

No matter how much you try to please God with your life and your marriage, you will experience frustration and failure if you're working in your own power. The secret is to establish a dynamic relationship with God.

This new commitment of your life to God will enrich your marriage. Sharing with your spouse what you've committed to is a powerful step in solidifying this commitment. As you exhibit the Holy Spirit's work within you, your spouse may be drawn to make the same commitment you've made. If both of you have given control of your lives to the Holy

Spirit, you'll be able to help each other remain true to God, and your marriage will be revolutionized. With God in charge of your lives, life becomes an amazing adventure!

Resources to Use as a Couple or in a Group

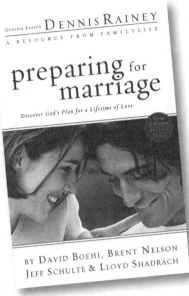

GENERAL EDITOR DENNIS RAINEY
A RESOURCE FROM FAMILYLIFE

preparing for marriage

Discover God's Plan for a Lifetime of Love

BY DAVID BOEHI, BRENT NELSON
JEFF SCHULTE & LLOYD SHADRACH

Preparing for Marriage
Discover God's Plan for a Lifetime of Love

It can be tempting, for couples who are engaged, to focus on planning their wedding day and ignore preparations for the lifetime commitment that begins after the cake is cut. Now, with this revised and updated edition of *Preparing for Marriage* from FamilyLife, couples can do both! Created by one of America's leading marriage and family ministries, this dynamic program is designed to help Christian couples lay the foundation for a strong, lasting and biblical marriage.

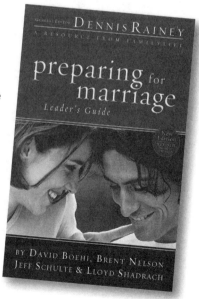

GENERAL EDITOR DENNIS RAINEY
A RESOURCE FROM FAMILYLIFE

preparing for marriage
Leader's Guide

BY DAVID BOEHI, BRENT NELSON
JEFF SCHULTE & LLOYD SHADRACH

Preparing for Marriage Leader's Guide

arried couples begin their lives together with a vow of
elong love and devotion . . . but many walk down the aisle
naware of all that promise entails. Now you can help en-
ged couples make their vows with open eyes and hearts,
lly prepared for the hard and rewarding work of building
strong and lasting Christian marriage.

s a supplement to *Preparing for Marriage*, the *Pre-
ring for Marriage Leader's Guide* is an invaluable
ol for pastors, premarital counselors, mentor couples
d small-group leaders. Inside is everything you need
help engaged couples establish a lasting relationship
ilt on an unshakeable foundation: Jesus Christ.

vailable at Bookstores Everywhere!

Devotions for Couples

Moments Together for Couples
Devotions for Drawing Near to God and
One Another

In the midst of the stress and pressure of everyday
life, *Moments Together for Couples* will give you
and your mate a chance to pause, relax and draw
upon the strength of the Lord. This easy-to-use
devotional helps you set aside anywhere from
5 to 30 minutes every day with your spouse to
grow closer to God and closer to each other.

Moments with You
Daily Connections for Couples

What is the true secret to spiritual growth for couples? Dennis and Barbara Rainey know from experience that the secret is more moments together. When you are lifting up your relationship and the rest of your life together to God, you won't be able to keep the spiritual growth from happening. In the pages of *Moments with You*, the Raineys offer just what couples need to get started or to continue growing in their quiet times together. These short but poignant biblical devotions are enjoyable and easy to use, providing a daily discussion point, prayer and Scripture reference. Married couples desiring a deeper spiritual connection with God and their spouse will come to treasure their time spent over *Moments with You*. For married couples of all ages and at all stages of life.

Available at Bookstores Everywhere!

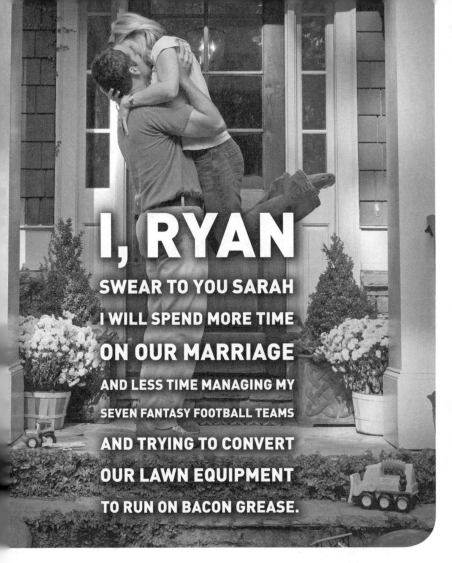

I, RYAN

SWEAR TO YOU SARAH
I WILL SPEND MORE TIME
ON OUR MARRIAGE
AND LESS TIME MANAGING MY
SEVEN FANTASY FOOTBALL TEAMS
AND TRYING TO CONVERT
OUR LAWN EQUIPMENT
TO RUN ON BACON GREASE.

rn how to fulfill your vows. At the Weekend to Remember
age getaway, you can put aside life's daily distractions and focus on each other.
ver 35 years we've helped couples learn how to build a strong and healthy
age. It's a perfect opportunity for premarried or newly-married couples to
e the potential in their relationship.

FAMILYLIFE presents
weekend to
remember